# MATTERING PRESS

Mattering Press is an academic-led Open Access publisher that operates on a not-for-profit basis as a UK registered charity. It is committed to developing new publishing models that can widen the constituency of academic knowledge and provide authors with significant levels of support and feedback. All books are available to download for free or to purchase as hard copies. More at matteringpress.org.

The Press's work has been supported by: Centre for Invention and Social Process (Goldsmiths, University of London), European Association for the Study of Science and Technology, Hybrid Publishing Lab, infostreams, Institute for Social Futures (Lancaster University), Open Humanities Press, and Tetragon.

## MAKING THIS BOOK

Mattering Press is keen to render more visible the unseen processes that go into the production of books. We would like to thank Uli Beisel and Michaela Spencer, who acted as the Press' coordinating editors for this book, the two reviewers Frida Hastrup and Dirk Postma, Jenn Tomomitsu for the copy-editing, Tetragon for the production and typesetting, Sarah Terry for the proofreading, and Ed Akerboom and infostreams for formatting the html versions of this book.

## COVER

Mattering Press thanks Łukasz Dziedzic for Lato, our incomparable cover typeface. It remains one of the best free typefaces available and is released by his foundry tyPoland under the free, libre and open source Open Font License.

Cover art by Julien McHardy.

# IMAGINING CLASSROOMS

*Stories of children,*
*teaching, and ethnography*

## VICKI MACKNIGHT

MATTERING PRESS

ISBN: 978-0-9931449-6-7 (pbk)
ISBN: 978-0-9931449-7-4 (ebk)

Mattering Press has made every effort to contact copyright holders and will be glad to rectify, in future editions, any errors or omissions brought to our notice.

# CONTENTS

# LIST OF ILLUSTRATIONS

# ON LOSING FOUNDATIONS

EXACTLY NINE MONTHS BEFORE I FINISHED THIS BOOK, I FELL PREGNANT. The falling took place in the contingent depths of my own body. Suddenly my queasy stomach and my exhausted spirit were in control. At first I would get myself to the library but spend my time working out the quickest way to the bathrooms. Then the bus ride became too much. Now my days were spent at home, sitting on a soft chair or crouched over the toilet bowl or flat out in bed. My vegetable garden began to wither and die because the idea of standing up and walking into the outside heat was too much. I chose food not on how it would taste going down, but on what it would be like when it almost inevitably came back up. I found myself impressed at the reckless way my partner would just drink a glass of water straight down. I did no work.

I think what happened is that I had lost the sense of my body being a firm foundation from which to live my life. I was used to my mind being clear, my body unnoticeable, and the first ruling the second effortlessly. But my mind had become fuzzy, my body immovable, and the domination of one by the other something that even my strongest effort of will couldn't achieve. What had happened was that the relations within my body – linking throat to stomach and stomach to brain – had become unstable and hence obvious. I began to understand what Iris Marion Young meant when she said that Western metaphysics, and its assumption of firm foundations, is based on the male body that does not change, does not bleed (Young 2005: 57, 107). I was learning in a most corporeal way that the world is not so fixed, and is ever in flux. It takes effort – and luck – to make the world seem to hold still.

And then my son was born. A perfectly normal human baby, at the beginning of his life he could not focus his eyes and he didn't realise his hands were his own. After a while he could punch himself in the face, and then could avoid punching himself in the face and put his hands into his mouth instead. He could stare at a toy suspended above him, and hit it. And, most thrilling, he could see me smiling at him and smile in return. He was learning to relate parts of his body together, to relate them to the material world, and to relate himself to the social world.

Like all of us, my son was born into a chaotic world ever in flux. He could sense no pattern. But we learn to make order. As he grew he gradually learnt a particular set of motions common to humans that enable us to impose ourselves upon the world. Our motions are regular, and we come to discern and expect regularities in the physical and social world. We throw a ball up, we catch it as it comes down. We see rain on a sunny day and look for rainbows. We find that if we are cruel, then others will be cruel in return. We learn to perform our bodies in ways that help us to recognise and create order. We learn to act in ways that are effective amongst our material and social partners.

These performances of ordering are deeply entwined with our ability to know. What we know is how to act to find and use patterns. We know how to interact with the world and to predict what will happen when we do so. My son learnt to hit the toys hanging above him in his baby gym. He learnt that when he does so they will swing back and forth like a pendulum. Later he will learn to see this same motion in playground swings, and he will learn to stretch and retract his body in order to control the swing. He will learn, physically, if not abstractly, that a ball describes the same curve when thrown. He will throw and catch unthinkingly. Later still, if he is better at mathematics than his mother, he will learn to draw parabolic curves from the numbers written on the board by a teacher. In all these cases he is learning ways to create a certain pattern in the world – the parabola – and, perhaps more impressively, to usefully predict its next element. In all these cases, what he knows are ways to effectively interact with the worlds of baby gyms and classrooms. He knows how to *do*: to hit, swing, catch, and map; to move, predict, and abstract.

This is one way of reading what the world is like, and how, therefore, we know about it. It is a particular theory on which to build a metaphysics and an epistemology and it is the theoretical approach of this book. Ian Hacking (1983) expressed this view very well. To Hacking the real is not something static that we represent, but something that we come to know through our interactions with it. From babyhood we come to know the real by using it to pull ourselves to our feet and stand on. Embodied creatures, we pull the real, and push it, and learn what happens. 'Reality,' Hacking teaches us, 'has to do with causation and our notions of reality are formed from our abilities to change the world' (Hacking 1983: 146; see also Verran 2001, chapter eleven).

When I became pregnant, the certainty that my body would behave and that my time was my own collapsed. It was only then that I began to truly understand the work of Ian Hacking, Annemarie Mol, Helen Verran, John Law, and other scholars I draw on here. In metaphysics they believe in there is no fixed is-ness, no foundation that we float above. We do not simply find ways to represent and read a stable world. Instead the world is made up of the relations we have with its objects as time flows on. Knowledge, as I learnt watching my son, is our ability to relate ourselves to a greater or lesser number of objects more or less successfully. Knowledge, in Verran's words, is relational (Verran 2001: 33–36). It is caught up in our performances in and of the world. For Verran, 'good' knowledge is that which enables us to act 'well' with the world, whatever that might mean.

Imagination is part of our performance of the world; it is part of the way we make ourselves related to objects and other people. It is how we think forward to predict, how we empathise with others to know a little of their ways of seeing and acting; it is how we play so that we can practise relating when the stakes are low. It is how we are able to think new thoughts, to ask, and create new objects. My questions here are about how imagination is done, specifically in primary school classrooms around Melbourne, Australia, and what this means for 'good' knowing and 'good' acting for children, teachers, and ethnographers.

# ACKNOWLEDGEMENTS

THANK YOU TO HELEN VERRAN, MY SUPERVISOR AT THE UNIVERSITY OF Melbourne. Without her guidance and support this project would have looked entirely different and much less.

Thank you to the group of graduate students gathered around Helen, including Christian Clark, Stephanie Lavau, Alison Marlin, and Michaela Spencer. Workshops and conversations with you all have always been stimulating.

Staff and students in the Departments of History and Philosophy of Science and Philosophy at the University of Melbourne and the Department of Anthropology at the University of Sydney were good friends and colleagues.

Examiners Estrid Sørensen and Lisa Adkins, reviewers Frida Hastrup, Dirk Postma and two anonymous reviewers all gave up their time to give valuable feedback.

Lynne Allen was kind enough to read and provide a teacher's perspective.

Everyone at Mattering Press has been hugely helpful, especially Uli Beisel.

Zach Weber – thank you. And Oskar and Edgar, this book is for you.

# INTRODUCTION

IN 2010, *NEWSWEEK* RAN THE COVER STORY 'CREATIVITY IN AMERICA: THE Science of Innovation and how to Re-ignite our Imaginations'. The article inside, by Po Bronson and Ashley Merryman, claimed that students in the United States are becoming less creative as shown by Torrance test scores, a metric developed in the 1950s. The cause, the authors suggest, might be too much TV and too little time for creativity at school. The solution? To turn to neuroscience. Teaching experts should develop tasks to encourage children to practise moving from left to right hemisphere thinking during the school day. The authors call on readers' fears of national decline by pointing out that in other nations, notably Britain, Australia, and China, creativity is part of the national school curriculum. But not so in America. The premise is clear: only by engineering creative thinking at schools can America deal with the coming economic and environmental challenges. 'The problems we face now, and in the future, simply demand that we do more than just hope for inspiration to strike' (Newsweek 19 July 2010: 49).

Schoolchildren's imagination, or more specifically the lack of it, is here presented as a public problem (Addelson 1993; Marres 2005). It is a concern for the future: for American predominance, for the global environment, for economically productive invention. The solution presented (as well as the measure of failure) is 'scientific'. Imaginations have been counted in Torrance tests and will be improved by linking left and right brain hemispheres more frequently in classroom practice.

Here is another way the public problem of imagination is presented:

> If we want this generation of children to make a difference, then we have
> to teach them to think outside of what have been the formal parameters

that we generally take as real. They need to see the world from a whole other point of view, because they've got a lot of fixing to do. So to be able to see economics from a new perspective; to be able to see how to deal with the world's waste; to deal with social and cultural boundaries in a new way, so that things like terrorism [...] just would not make any sense [...] It's about finding new ways to deal with this world as it is, and I don't think my generation has any longer any capacity for that – otherwise I reckon we'd be doing it (Author interview with teacher, Steiner School, 15 June 2007).

These are the words of Shirley, a teacher of nine-year-olds at a Steiner school in Melbourne, Australia (above and in what follows referred to simply using the pseudonym 'Steiner School'. Other schools are referred to using similar terms). She also sees imagination as the solution to future crises – of economics, environments, and human conflicts. But her practices of imagination, as we shall see, make no mention of the brain's hemispheres. Her students' imaginations are made by storytelling, by deep emotional links to myths, and by concentrated reproductions of mental images.

Imagination is given as a solution to our collective problems. It can also be told as a solution to our personal problems. As another teacher put it,

I have come to understand the role of imagination is about being able to see endless possibilities and providing myself and others with different thinking of the possibilities and imagining, and understanding that if you can imagine yourself doing something you've got a greater chance of actually achieving it (Government School, author interview with teacher, 29 May 2007).

We could say that different people think about imagination differently. They can see it as a matter of brain function, or emotional connections to visual images, or providing oneself with a new path in life. But we should not rest there. I will argue that imagination does not simply look different from different perspectives. Rather, *different imaginations are made though different practices*:

The kids play a game each day at lunchtime; most of the class are involved in some way. They have gathered a bunch of sticks and made it into a little house, or sometimes it's a boat, or an animal's den. Each child has an animal name, one they have invented or been granted. As they play they take on roles – cooking, building a fireplace, adventuring along the fence line – that they do alone or with others. One girl is on the outs. They said she can play, but that she has to be wombat. Lumbering old wombat, and while she wants to play she doesn't want to be wombat. Nevertheless, she goes and gets pine needles from the other side of the playground to make a bed, and when she lays them in a soft, prickly pile at the back of the house, the others are interested. They lie down with her.

This girl is a skilful user of imagination: turning pine needles into a bed, and her wombat self into a cosy, sleeping thing. By doing so, she also re-makes – for now at least – her relationships with her peers. Imagination in this game is obviously being done with materials (pine needles), words and labels (wombat), bodies (that adventure and lie down), and social relations (children first at odds and now lying together). The imagination children use here could not be separated from these material things; it could not stand alone as some pure imagination. These events are not just happening in someone's mind, and if they were, nothing in this girl's social world would change. The materiality of imagination can be obvious in play, and less obvious in a classroom lesson. But, I will argue, it is important that we work to see that in classrooms too, imagination is *done*.

Key to this book is the understanding that imagination is not an abstract, ephemeral, mental object. Minds have a lot to do with imagination, of course. But so do bodies (that play, draw, speak, write, and touch) and so do other more mundane objects (pens and papers, huts and hoops, books and audiovisual materials). Imaginations are practised, they are done by embodied minds and clever bodies, with other bodies, and with stuff that is physically present, remembered, or fantasised. Imaginations might be habits: patterns that minds and bodies have done before. Or they might be newly improvised, blending people and materials in novel ways. Some imaginative practices might be praised by teachers and/or peers, while others might be ignored or hidden or told to stop. Each imaginative practice will make certain things possible and other things not possible.

Teaching philosophies are at least partly about these possibilities: what we want possible for children to be able to do and to think in their future. Teachers working at different kinds of schools, in different communities of parents, with different curricula, and with different understandings of what children are, have different teaching philosophies. Their values and aspirations for children vary, and they seek to achieve these, in part, by mobilising children's imaginations. What is imagination in Steiner practice and in practices at a special school? How important is it? What is it most importantly for? How is imagination done differently than, say, at a Catholic school?

The children I worked with were aged eight, nine, and ten, in grade four classrooms (or grade three/four classrooms). Their classrooms were in Melbourne, Australia. Each was in one of five schools with a specific teaching philosophy, a social community, and a set of needs. One was at a Steiner school. These are run in accordance with the ideas (as they are now interpreted) of Rudolf Steiner, a late nineteenth-century philosopher and spiritualist. Another was at an 'independent' school, one that does not have to follow government curriculum on account of collecting running costs from parents as well as the government. In this case the fees were high, and most parents correspondingly wealthy. A third classroom was at a government school, or one run by state government money and with state government curriculum. The fourth school was for children with low IQs and assorted cognitive disorders. This 'special' school was located in the low-income outskirts of Melbourne. The final school was likewise in a low-income area but was primarily for the children of Catholic families. Each of these schools, and these classrooms, had different goals for what children should ideally become. These goals are linked in complex ways to the community of parents, to the educational tradition of the school, and to the ideas of the individuals who work there. Along with all these differences, in each classroom imagination was being *done* differently.

## 'Doing'

I say 'done'. This shows a concern with materiality and practice I share with the theoretical world of Science and Technology Studies (STS), and more specifically a corner of that world. STS is a very divided discipline, as shown, among other things, by various uses of the apparently shared word 'ontology' (see Van Heur et al. 2012; and Woolgar et al. 2012). The community of STS scholars I see myself as part of have worked hard to show us materiality in practice in various places: scientific labs, hospitals, fish farms, markets, schools, and more (Latour 1988; Callon 1998; Mol 2002; Sørensen 2009; Law 2012). In all these places, people use materials in particular ways and these ways generate particular objects. These objects may be multiple. Some may be standardised and some may be 'othered'. Each set of practices has implications, whether it be for people, fish, diseased legs, or knowledge cultures. Each has implications for how things could be done in the future. In this type of STS work, we are given analyses of how things are done now, what multiple objects are generated by this doing, and hopefully, space is made for things that might be otherwise lost, sidelined, or terminated.

It is important, I think, to point out that this is not a form of relativism. By this I mean that it is not saying that different people *see* the world differently. This, as Helen Verran points out, would be to continue to assume that there is a 'real world' at the base of all our experiences that can, nevertheless, be seen differently. She calls this a 'foundationalist' assumption that moves us hardly further than universalism from belief in a single, real, true knowledge. Both universalism and relativism assume a separation between knower and world that can only be bridged inadequately by our representations of it (Verran 2001: 31–36). Good knowledge about the foundational world, whether in universalist or relativist modes, would be that which came closest to *representing* the world.

Verran presents instead a metaphysics that tells the 'real' as multiple and emergent in practice. Knowers, that is to say, exist in 'communities of practice [that are] creative and generative' (Verran 2001: 29). Objects and knowledge could not be made just any way, because how the real is made is constrained by the physical, material, and social locations of knowers. This means that our options for understanding, and for other acts in practice, are always 'more than one, but this does not mean they are fragmented into being many' (Mol 2002: viii; from Strathern 1991: 35).

'Good knowing' in this new metaphysics is not a question of which representations come closest to the 'real', but of what enables knowers to best *intervene* in
the world. This is a notion of knowing that Ian Hacking articulates nicely. He says

> [r]eality has to do with causation and our notions of reality are formed from
> our abilities to change the world [...] We shall count as real what we can use
> to intervene in the world to affect something else, or what the world can use
> to affect us' (1983: 146).

Our question then becomes one that feminist philosophers, among others, have
tackled. What are 'good' ways of intervening in the world? The 'good' cannot
be something we can define as fixed and for always, because 'goodness' will
emerge from responses to whatever is going on. Kathryn Pyne Addelson, for
example, calls human lives 'passages of discovery and creation' and is interested
in how we might most ethically follow them (Addelson 1994: 1). In this picture, morality and ethics are not fixed already, waiting for the analyst to define
or uncover, but rather emerge 'out of people's interactions [...] moral explanation (and the categories of explanation) are constructed in social interactions'
(Addelson 1991: 83).

What Verran, Addelson, and others give us, then, is an ontology (that the *real*
is generated in practice), an epistemology (that we *know* when we are able to act
effectively with other agents and materials), and an ethics (that *good* knowing
means acting in better, rather than worse, ways for other agents and materials).
This is what I will call a non-foundational or relational way of understanding, a
*relational metaphysics*. This has implications for what good research and writing
will look like, and we shall see this soon.

But first, a couple of quick examples might help this make sense. First, Verran.
She tells a story in her 2001 *Science and an African Logic* of teaching maths
teachers in Nigeria. As part of her job, she helped design and observe maths
lessons in Yoruba classrooms. There she was confused. The lessons that went
as she had designed them often failed to engage the students. They were unable
to grasp the subject matter of maths. But when teachers left the script and did
the lesson 'wrong', they seemed to teach the children effectively. She gives us

an example of two lessons on length done by measuring the students' heights. The first used a metre ruler to measure, a way of understanding extension that is commonplace in Western settings. But this only generated confusion. The second used small cards with string wrapped round and round. The children engaged cheerfully and effectively, even though this seems like the wrong way to think about extension.

So, Verran wondered, how to explain this? She could explain this as relativism – that Western and Yoruba mathematics see the world differently. Then the ethical response would be to respect the Yoruba teaching and give them resources to sometimes move into Western mathematics. Students could then switch between the two depending on their needs. But this would reinforce the gap between Yoruba and Western knowledge, and habits and people. Better, she argues, as well as closer to the empirical experience, to value moments when Western and Yoruba knowledge-making practices are done in new ways, generating new combined knowledges (Verran 2001: 1–29).

We can also look at the work of Annemarie Mol, who has long been concerned with human bodies and how they are made in multiple ways in medical practices (Mol 2002; Mol and Law 2004; Mol 2008). In a recent piece (2012), she takes this interest into the world of Dutch dieting advice. When dieticians give advice about ways to lose weight they appeal to different ways we practise what bodies are. Are they unruly pleasure seekers that need to be disciplined by a rational mind? This body would be done by counting calories. Or are they ancient machines long evolved to desire what is bad for their modern instantiations? These bodies should be done by limiting sugar and fat. Or are they part of a culture where plates have traditionally been divided one way and should be divided another? These bodies should be done by putting more vegetables and fewer carbohydrates on plates. These ways of understanding and doing bodies are what Mol calls ontonorms (a word mixing ontology and normativity), though she is careful to say that this term is not a theory. As she explains it, '"ontonorms" is a methodological *tool*. My hope is that it may sensitise us to materialities and issues of good and bad at the same time' (2012: 381, italics added). As we shall see later, we might call a tool like this a 'sensitising concept' (Blumer 1954). The kinds of questions we should ask with ontonorms are about politics, about what is good and bad for bodies, and what might be better. She gives us the alternative mode of dieting by 'enjoying your food'. Bodies, food, and their relationships are re-imagined here, positively, making space for a new way of doing 'good' bodies.

These two authors give us possibilities: different ways to value mathematical practices and new imaginaries for doing 'good' eating. They are possibilities that exist with and against other possibilities, ones that we are more familiar with: dividing Yoruba from Western mathematics, and diets based on conventional advice about counting calories, allowing only occasional treats, and rearranging your plate.

There are conventional imaginations too, or better and worse ways of talking about and doing imagination. The call to do imagination by closing your eyes and picturing something is likely familiar to readers. So too, the imagination where you make something creative in drama or in art. Or the imagination where you put yourself into another person's shoes and walk around. I will show how these imaginations are done in primary school classrooms, because they are being done there and they are important and interesting.

But I do not jump from these conventional imaginations to ask a conventional question about what imagination 'really is', because as I will argue, imagination is enacted in multiple practices. I don't ask questions about what is necessary for a practice to count as imaginative, nor do I claim that some imaginations are more 'imaginative' than others. This is to say that I do not do a type of philosophy that searches for essences (see Warnock 1976; White 1990). Nor am I interested in what goes on in minds as imaginative tasks are done. This counts me out of psychology and philosophy of mind (see Kosslyn 1994; Frawley 1997; Currie and Ravenscroft 2002; McGinn 2004). Nor am I concerned with the (important) question of access to education and to powerful knowledge (Moore and Muller 1999; Moore and Young 2001; Young 2008. For an extended discussion, see Macknight, 2011a).

I want to tell about the multiple possibilities for doing imagination that I see in classrooms. What about other ways of perspective-taking, seeing 'with' and 'for' otherness? What about imagination to help relationships make sense and work? What about imagination for making connections between disparate pieces of information? What about the imaginations ethnographers themselves use to make definitions, to make classes and categories, and for doing ethical analysis? These possible imaginations are ones I will describe as being done in practice, by teachers, by students, and by ethnographers. They are generated in practice, in relation to various materials, shaped by people with complex and varying notions of what is and what should be.

## Locating and Writing

I was already interested in primary schools' imaginations when I noticed a concern with the lack of imagination in young people. I had first become interested in imagination being used in an Australian primary school curriculum from the 1930s. There it was done as a particular type of empathy in the hope this would prevent a future world war. After this failed, a new curriculum was written in the 1950s that used imagination in quite different ways to teach children to identify with their fellow Australians. This was an imagination of networked relations (see Macknight 2007, 2008, 2010). So I knew about imaginations in Victorian primary schools from a specific past. I knew about the profound levels on which imagination was to work: in forming identities, moralities, and futures. But I did not know about how imagination was being done now – in this specific time and place. So I set out to learn.

To get to one school, I walked. Two were close enough that I rode my bike, and two were so far I caught a suburban train. Surrounding the schools were (variously) an arts precinct, a leafy park, a private boys' high school, well-maintained suburban houses, a set of scummy shops, and a tract of newly developed homes near a strip mall. Obviously, but easy to forget, these schools are physically located in place and in time. Their physical location links to their social location: communities of parents with various amounts of money, various values and ambitions for their children, various visions of what 'good' education is.

They were also located in more subtle ways. Each counted itself into an educational tradition, selectively reiterating values and practices that lead backwards into the past. We find out something of the educational tradition they belong to by asking about their funding structures and the fees they charge, by reading the documents they prepare for parents, and by noticing whether the children wear blazers, or polo shirts, or no uniform at all. To most Western observers the fact that a child calls their teacher by their first name will locate the school in a progressive educational tradition, while a child calling their teacher 'sir' will do the opposite. The state makes itself present here too, in various guises, appearing as curricula content, modes of assessment, and forms of professional develop-ment. The state is here in the very buildings it has fully or partially funded, the pay of teachers, child-to-teacher ratios, and many other things.

In each school, too, is the world (mostly the European and American world), brought by 'international' educational and psychological theories. This is research and theory that teachers have been taught at university or training college, that they read in curricula, and learn in professional development courses.

So these classrooms are located in Melbourne and, at the same time, they are located in the Western traditions of educational policy, funding, and practice. They are local and global in very concrete ways (Hastrup and Fog Olwig 1994; Mol 2004). They can be made both local and global in another way too. I can choose to write about the classrooms in local terms, focusing on the particular children and teachers I meet, and on the ways they operate. And I can write in analytic terms, taking the children and teachers out of their particular places and telling them in relation to theories developed in North America and Europe, by educationalists, sociologists, psychologists, and myriad others. Children and teachers can be told as related to each other or to analytic frames. The 'local' then is not just a place or a set of people and practices, but also a way of writing. Likewise the 'global' is not a place, certainly not a place that just encompasses the local, but a way of relating and telling. In this book, I try to locate classrooms as both local and global, particular and general.

Using a personal voice is part of this strategy. It is for reminding readers that it was 'I' who was there, really there, sometimes confused, sometimes excited. I will not hide behind the language of objective fact because if we listen to feminist epistemologists, objective facts are situated ones. They are seen from the bodies we, of necessity, inhabit (Haraway 1988; Alcoff and Potter 1993; Harding 2004 [1993]). Moreover, there is no such thing as knowing except from the position of a body. Using the first person, 'I', is for resisting the easy forgetting that it takes work to turn the empirical into the analytical, the specific into the general, and that this work too could be done differently.

The world, knowledge, and knower are not separate in practice, but are only separated in the ongoing work of analysing and representing. Writing is part of this ongoing separation work, and therefore texts are part of the way academics practise in the world. Taking a broad interest in social science methods, John Law argues against the rigidity of accounts of method that insist that there are correct ways to research and write about the world. Instead he advocates 'methods that are quieter and more generous' (Law 2004: 15). According to Law, we need methods that remember that we come to know by being human participants in human worlds that are not governed by rules for knowing some assumed 'out there' from a distance. Nor, likewise, should there be any single correct way to write because to write is to communicate specifics of what it is like to be here or there. As he puts it, 'method does not "report" on something that is already there. Instead, in one way or another, it makes things different. The issue becomes how to make things different and what to make' (Law 2004: 143).

Working and writing in this way is not part of the reflexive turn of the 1980s, described as the navel-gazing of the self-centred scholar (Pinch 1988; for a more positive take, see Ashmore 1989; Ashmore and Woolgar 1988). Instead, it is a way to remember that knowledge is always located in bodies and that writing is not simply reporting. Moreover, it is a way to give symmetry to my accounts: if the nature of imagination is that it is performed and if teachers and children are performing imagination, then so too are ethnographers. Ethnographers, like teachers and children, should be described as having the capacity to perform imaginations in multiple ways.

## Finding Imaginations

In the book that follows, I present five ways to practise imaginations which I see as distinct. Each is important in a particular classroom, but this is not to say that it is the only imagination being done. Nor is it to say that there are no other ways of doing imagination beyond these five. I present these five, and each to a chapter, for two reasons. One is the simple need for coherence and tidiness. Multiplicity, complexity, mess – all exist in practice, but in practice, as we all know, it can often be difficult to work out what is going on.

The second reason to present five distinct imaginations is to be of assistance to practitioners: teachers, parents, others who work with children, educational theorists, curriculum designers, ethnographers, and anyone else who may wish to explore the possibilities of their own imaginative practice.

As such, I present the five imaginations as 'sensitising concepts'. Taking this term from Blumer (1954), I wish to point out, as he did, the difference between 'definitive' and 'sensitising' concepts:

> A definitive concept refers precisely to what is common to a class of objects, by the aid of a clear definition in terms of attributes or fixed bench marks [...] A sensitising concept lacks such specification of attributes or bench marks [...] Whereas definitive concepts provide prescriptions of what to see, sensitising concepts merely suggest directions along which to look [...] They rest on a general sense of what is relevant (1954: 7).

As I worked to discern imagination in its multiplicity, I tried very hard not to have a preconceived notion of what imagination is. When I went into classrooms I didn't know what I would see, and I tried to notice imagination in its broad and multiple doings. Obvious were times when teachers or children said the word 'imagination'. What practices were they labelling for me? I also used the teachers' own accounts of their values to guide my analysis. To take them seriously is to do justice to their ambitions for the children they devote their days to. Obvious too were the moments that puzzled me, times when connections were made that I simply didn't really follow. This happened, for example, when children showed me workbooks that said their fingers were like the stars. How was imagination mobilised for this to make sense to children? (Verran 1999). But these were not the only practices I saw as important. I also worked to notice things that happened repeatedly, patterns and clumps of practices that seemed to have to do with imagination. If, for example, the teacher wrote a starter sentence on the board for creative writing each day, and each day forbade certain subjects and words, then each day in creative writing imagination was simultaneously mobilised and constrained in very particular ways.

In observing and taking part in these classrooms, being attentive to the work being done, the words used, the surprises felt, and the habits reiterated, and then working as an analyst shaping and presenting this text, I have tried to catch something of how imagination is being taught and done in different ways. I have also looked for careful ways of describing the differing imaginations which I have encountered and write about, so as to do justice to this ethnographic material while also generating a collection of imaginations which might be helpful for others. In other words, my types are *tools*, sensitising concepts to help us notice and know. It just happens that we – teachers, children, myself, and hopefully readers – feel comfortable to call all these sets of practices 'imagination'. It is interesting, this, and shows again the useful vagueness of language that it can hold so many practices together.

## CHAPTER OUTLINE

This book tells several interlinked stories. All of them are set in primary schools in Melbourne, Australia, and at desks shortly afterwards. All concern the imagination of teachers, children, and ethnographers. And all are part of an attempt to show ways of enacting imagination in classrooms and considering how 'good' imagination and 'good' teaching might be done in non-foundational or relational ways.

One string holding the book together is contained in the figure of the imaginative ethnographer. This ethnographer is learning to do ethnography in classrooms, looking always at the practices that make real and commonplace what we normally think of as an abstract mental category. She is learning to watch and listen and categorise, to think and imagine, in new ways. She is learning to work with non-foundational terms and begins the tricky work of managing categories as contingent outcomes.

These are the stories I start with. They are about how ethnographers and the rest of us think about classrooms (and other research sites), about data analysis, and about definitions. They are about how to reimagine these things so that we might become better about thinking and acting in classrooms, doing analysis, and defining imagination. These first chapters frame and explain the more empirically focused chapters in part two. I hope that people who are interested in theory and in doing ethnography might really enjoy these first chapters, but skipping straight to the second part and returning to part one is always an option.

So these first three chapters ask what thinking with a relational metaphysics might mean for how social researchers think about their own knowledge practices. First, I wonder about how to re-conceptualise the object of our knowledge. What are social groups, or more specifically, what are classrooms? I suggest that they can be usefully understood both as units that nest within other, larger units, and as ordered and ordering assemblages. I use the notion of 'classed and classing bodies' to point out that students, teachers, and researchers are part of ongoing processes of classifying each other and the world more generally.

In chapter two, I think about definitions: how we define imagination and how we think about definitions themselves. I argue that we generally think of meaning as something fixed and singular, where we might better think of it as being multiple because it is done in practice. Meanings, I say, are conglomerations of our practices, sticking together in particular ways because of our backgrounds, our beliefs and aims, and our work. We will see this through how our five teachers talk about what imagination is.

Next I extend these questions to wonder about the practice of classifying research materials: in this case the pictures children drew for me under the heading of 'a time I used my imagination'. I argue here that researchers' analytic practices are bodily and habitual. But with their bodily imagination a researcher can find new ways of ordering their information and this makes for different theoretical claims. I suggest that these claims should be assessed not in terms of truth, but in terms of ethics. Putting materials into different orders, after all, does not change their truthfulness, but it does change the work our accounts might do in the world. This again is to make a link between how we know and how we live.

I do not claim to have the solution to the public problem of teaching imagination as if there were only one for all times and places. But I do have my stories about how imagination is framed and developed with children in practice, and

I have claims to make about which are better and worse for living in the world as I envision it to be. This is done through the order of chapters in part two. I begin with stories of what I name as 'representational imagination' being done at a Steiner school. This imagination is foundational by its nature, encouraging children to form pictures in their minds of the 'really real', then find ways to make physical copies of these pictures. Deep within these practices is the platonic divide between the real world and human knowing of it. This divide also lies deep in our understandings of what ethnographic truth and ethics are. I explore how we might aim beyond representation in the conclusion of this chapter.

I then move in chapter five to a high-fee-paying independent school, where imagination seems to be done as ways to perform oneself as an imaginative and humorous person. Children are to act imaginatively, but not imaginatively in just any way they like. For all creative performers, I suggest, some form of discipline is required. This can be discipline of time, bodies, sounds, or creative processes. Discipline is essential if imagination is to transform things in the ways intended.

We turn next to the imagination practised at a middle-class, suburban, government school. Here, children are taught to take the perspectives of others in ways I initially assumed were intended as empathetic. I gradually noticed, however, that children were not successfully seeing the world with the eyes, or from the shoes, of others. Moreover, I gradually came to realise that the teacher was not aiming for this limited form of perspective-taking, but for something broader and more flexible. This is an account of the range of ways we can do and think about perspective-taking. This moves us beyond a relativist stance that says there are multiple views of the world that we can jump between. Instead we are working towards a relational account of imagining, an account that is extended in the chapter that follows.

In this seventh chapter we focus on a classroom at a special school for low-IQ students. Here, where children are described as dangerously self-involved, imagination is practised as ways of relating oneself to others. These are techniques by which children are to recognise that others have hopes and needs. Imaginative scenarios are used to show children that by imagining together more can be achieved. It is in the practices of imaginatively interacting (even at the low levels achieved by these students) that we begin to find relational imagining being done.

In the conclusion, we move from practices of imagining that aim primarily at social knowing and living to those that aim for conceptual knowing. Starting with the practices of the teacher at a Catholic school in a low-income area, here we look at imagination as making connections between pieces of information. We then ask what habitual modes of connection-making look like at the other four schools. Again this is a story that moves us from foundational to relational types of knowledge-making, though now the knowledge in question is more conceptual than social. This is a conclusion that shows how we might imagine as relational thinkers.

I return to questions about the future in the afterword. There I wonder what the stories I tell might do in the world. I wonder about how the multiple imaginations I describe are related and how we might imagine relationships between multiple imaginations. I wonder about what parts of my account might travel best with my readers. It is a conclusion too, but in a more reflective mode.

The stories I tell are personal and imaginative, but at the same time they are as real as my abilities to notice and communicate can make them. I hope that from reading these stories, or some of them, readers might notice their own performances of imagination, and those of the people around them, and wonder afresh what they mean for good knowing and good living in the future.

# PART ONE

# IMAGINATION IN SOCIAL SCIENCE PRACTICE

# I

# IMAGINING CLASSROOMS

I am nervous. This is to be my first day in a classroom 'doing research', and I'm not sure what it's going to mean. I dress carefully; make sure all my forms and ethics clearances are in my bag; check again for my notebook. When I arrive at school, I find the right classroom and my teacher. I chat, trying to seem competent. When the bell rings, I am seated at the teacher's desk. I have to stand, surprised and flustered when he asks me to introduce myself to the kids. Why hadn't I predicted this was going to happen? I tell them who I am, and blunder through an explanation of what I'm doing here, what I'm going to be looking at. Geez, if I find this difficult to explain to children, how am I going to explain it in a book?

THIS PERHAPS MAKES ME SOUND FOOLISH, BLUNDERING. RESEARCHERS ARE supposed to know what they are doing; planning experiments, writing methodologies, organising teams. But in the social sciences, and likely in any sphere working with human participants and seeking qualitative information, the rules are not clear (Law 2004). One simply cannot know exactly what one is looking for until one finds it. This is a version of Meno's paradox: roughly, how can I search for knowledge about something if I do not know anything about that something? To solve it we need a theory of knowledge that admits to imperfect knowledge (Dillon 1997: 1–2). We have to blunder a little. But at the same time we need to be able to tell our participants which parts of their lives we are hoping to take for our texts. And so we strike a paradox: I am expected to be certain about what I am looking for (seeking a specific truth), but the unfamiliarity of the community of practice I find myself in demands that I be flexible, open, and responsive to what is there.

I was able to be in these classrooms only because I had successfully given an account of what I was going to do and what I thought I might learn. These are a requirement of ethics procedures, of which I completed three – for the university, the state government, and the Catholic education office. On these forms, I said I would do ethnographic fieldwork for three weeks each in five grade four classrooms, or until I believed I had done sufficient research to stop noticing new things; conduct an audio-recorded semi-structured interview with the teacher; and ask that the children draw and write about 'a time they used their imaginations'. Explaining why this was an important topic, I had written about empathy and creativity. These were what I thought I might find. They were also what I thought would sound like persuasive rationale to primary school principals and teachers.

I presented these sure methodologies and serious-sounding rationales to schools. I gained access to some classrooms by ringing up or visiting school principals and others by following personal networks. I found that principals were hard to make contact with, but once they were on the end of a phone line or across a desk, they were decisive: very often interested but running too busy a school to wish for researchers. If they did agree, we entered into a process of negotiation over issues such as which teacher might be interested and suitable. Would I like to work with an experienced or a new teacher? On several occasions it seemed very obvious to the principal who would be best for me to work with: some teachers are understood by the principal, and indeed across the school, as being 'good at imagination'. For the principals in these discussions, it was the teacher who is the classroom.

At the end of these negotiations, I found myself in various classrooms. All were for grade four or three/four children. They were not necessarily the ones I would have chosen. They were the effect of who I asked and how I presented myself. They were the effect of how far I could travel. They were the effect of the stresses of running a school; of a principal's sense that this could be interesting or useful to their teachers; or their belief that there was already a teacher who would show their school to be a richly imagining place. Each classroom was located in a different type of school: independent (or private), government (or state), Steiner (or Waldorf), Catholic, and special (for children with low IQs). They were located in different areas around Melbourne, from inner to outer city, in demographics that ranged from very wealthy to very poor (see Fig. 1). However, they were not, and never could be, representative of 'primary schools in Melbourne'. There are too many schools, divided across too many types of category. Each school, just like each individual, is uniquely situated in the wider social world. The schools I discuss, then, provide a *range*, not a sample.

But where am I? And what am I to do there?

**FIG. 1** Map of Melbourne to Show School Locations

This chapter is an attempt to answer these questions rephrased in the more general terms of 'what is a classroom?' and 'How should we think of the appropriate behaviours for a participant-observer?' Here I explore two answers to these questions. One set of answers presents classrooms as parts of a whole, and the other presents classrooms as complex assemblages. In giving each answer, I provide a description of these five classrooms. Importantly, each also differently directs what a participant-observation researcher should do in a classroom.

Readers might wonder how I can give two answers. Which one do I think correct? My suggestion is that the two answers are two ways of performing the analytic work of theorising. Perhaps more clearly, they are 'modes of ordering' done by your author. 'Modes of ordering' is the term used by sociologist John Law. They are what Law argues we use all the time in our physical, material, and discursive performances of reality. They are modes of relating subjects and objects in ways that are provisional and potentially multiple. They are what we perform with every time we engage with the world, including when doing qualitative research. Law explains that

> [T]hey are all of: stories; interpellations; knowing relations; materially heterogeneous sociotechnical arrangements; and discourses. This is because they run through and perform material relations, arrangements with a pattern and their own logic. Except [...] they are smaller. More contingent. Putatively less consistent, less coherent (Law 1994; Law 2000: 23).

I will suggest here two modes of ordering that I believe structure our engagement with classrooms, though it is laborious to become aware of these. Both were available to me when I entered classrooms and they remain available as I work to make sense of classrooms – as were many others. Now though, I can choose which is the best for my intervening. I choose to work with two, not because I think there are only two, but because I find them useful for thinking.

One mode takes classrooms to be nesting within schools, and schools nesting within 'society' (see figure 2). In the first part of this chapter, I will try

```
┌─────────────────────────────────────────────────────────┐
│                        SOCIETY                            │
│   ┌───────────────────────────────────────────────────┐  │
│   │                     SCHOOL                          │  │
│   │      ┌──────────────────────────────────────┐      │  │
│   │      │                                        │      │  │
│   │      │              CLASSROOM                 │      │  │
│   │      │                                        │      │  │
│   │      └──────────────────────────────────────┘      │  │
│   │                                                     │  │
│   └───────────────────────────────────────────────────┘  │
│                                                           │
│            COMMUNITY EDUCATIONAL TRADITION                │
└─────────────────────────────────────────────────────────┘
```

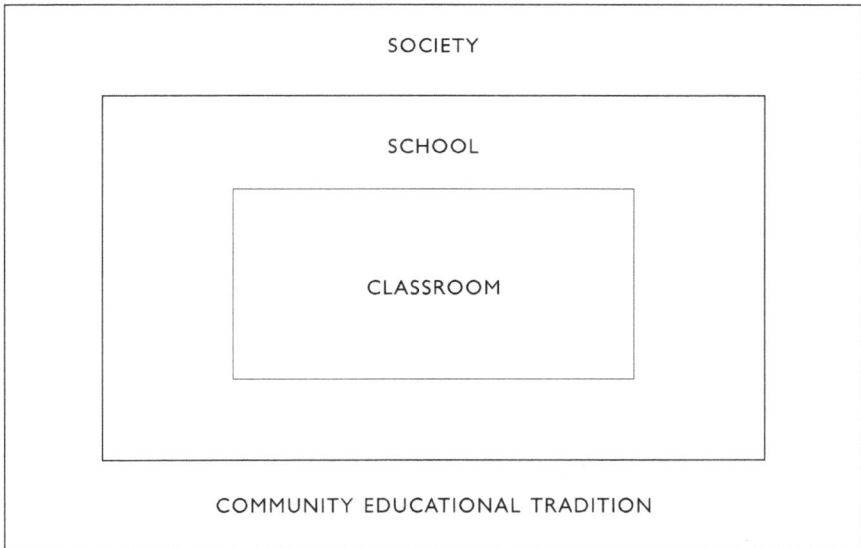

**FIG. 2** Diagram to show classroom nesting in school nesting in educational tradition

out a particular version of this idea using the work of Kieran Egan. But I will go a bit further. Instead of representing society or community or values, I will argue schools work hard to present and build an ideal (future) society within their own grounds. Pictured this way as bounded communities, the participant-observer should act as a respectful contributing member of these societies and their values. Giving up their own prejudices, they should seek to represent classrooms as isolated social fields within the broader field of society. This is a mode of ordering that makes classrooms part of schools which are part of society's ideal possibilities. This mode of ordering also makes researchers into those who are to report on, or perhaps judge, these 'societies'. To some extent this is how I acted in classrooms, and it forms part of what I do in writing. But I also follow a second mode of ordering.

This second mode takes classrooms to be assemblages of classed and classing bodies. Here I use the word 'class' to identify two important features of the persons gathered in a classroom and school. These are (1) that they are part of the wider social hierarchies of wealth, culture, and future potential, and (2) that they are bodies who are learning to classify their worlds in particular but everyday ways.* To draw together these two features, I speak of classed and classing bodies. When researchers, with their own classed and classing bodies, come to participate and observe in such places, they experience harmonies, clashes, and interruptions to their bodies. Their own values, springing from their belonging to a particular class, are mobilised. This impacts on how they are able to observe and participate. More, because their abilities to classify are tied to aspects of their class identities, they might find their descriptions of what was going on difficult to return to the academy. This mode of ordering makes classrooms sites where classed and classing bodies interact in harmonious and disruptive ways. This makes the researcher's subject position as one who works the uneven ground between classrooms, cultural and socio-economic class, and their own modes of classifying.

I tell about classrooms in both modes of ordering because both are useful for different purposes. The first tells readers the types of things they are accustomed to hearing about a couple of schools, educational traditions, and demographics. They serve to fit the classrooms into a way of ordering the world that we are familiar with. Using school information and marketing materials, the researcher represents classrooms as they seem to represent themselves. I tell the second because I believe it speaks more accurately and more ethically about what it is to do classroom research.

## WHAT IS A CLASSROOM?
## ANSWERING WITHIN THE SCHOOL-SOCIETY NEXUS

At the start of this chapter I found myself in a classroom. One answer I can provide to explain where I was is to say a classroom is a nesting part of a school and the school a nesting part of society. This seems quite natural: it is after all how we are used to thinking of our individual identities as persons in families that are in communities that are in cities that are in nation-states. Using this picture of classrooms we would ask about how they are related to society: to

---

* By using 'class' I don't mean to associate this work with complex Marxist theories, merely to point out the continued importance of social and economic hierarchies and the signifying social categories that result.

what educational traditions do their schools subscribe? How are they situated in terms of the demographics of wealth and social values they represent (and attract parents with)?

This initially would seem to claim something quite simple: that a Steiner classroom, for example, represents the values of the Steiner community. This needs to be complexified, for most classrooms represent a mixture of values that have been transmitted through time. The work of Kieran Egan will help us do so.

The school-in-society picture is one Egan implicitly uses in his book, *The Educated Mind* (1997). He tells of a way to pull apart the complex threads that make up educational traditions and goals. By a deep and rich understanding of (Western) society's hopes for schooling, Egan suggests that all schools represent some mixture of three aims. These are about what people are (and should be), and since agglomerations of people will form societies, these aims also evidently picture what society is (or should be). However, according to Egan, these three aims are inconsistent and this has created an insoluble problem for education. Only by developing a new vision of what learning is might schools escape this morass; or this is how he introduces the theory he articulates throughout this book.

Egan provides a way of distinguishing the educational aims that, he argues, (though inconsistent) guide schooling. These are (1) the aim to socialise children so that they will be good citizens of the society and polity; (2) the aim to provide the child with accurate and objective knowledge of the world around them; and (3) the aim to let children develop their individual human potential. Does it make sense to think of children educated to live as Christians developing objective knowledge about the world? Or to think of children learning to be objective and accurate but also happy to follow arbitrary social conventions? All three conflicting goals, he suggests, are present in all our schools in some mixture, with one generally appearing dominant (Egan 1997, especially chapter one).[*]

---

[*] A fuller rendering of his argument sees that this is only the set-up for an alternative theory of the role of schools, namely to advance children through a series of 'kinds of understanding' made possible by their (hopefully) increasing facility for oral and written language, while also minimising the losses associated with these changes in understanding.

I introduce Egan here to help us see clearly how some schools represent themselves and understand their distinct educational goal. For example, according to their own advertising material, Steiner Schools are described as aiming for the third objective outlined by Egan, which is developing the individual human potential of each child in spiritual and intellectual terms. As the Steiner School advertising flyer puts this, 'we aim to provide the right nourishment at each stage of physical, emotional and spiritual growth' and 'strive to allow children to fully experience the joys and mysteries of childhood' (Anonymous undated, 'Steiner School').

This goal does nest nicely within the values of particular segments of society. The words quoted above were printed on a flyer that interested parties are encouraged to pick up from a box outside the school gate. This gate is located in an arts precinct, so while the foot traffic is light, it is also made up of a specific self-selected demographic – those likely to already be interested in community organisations, personal artistic expression, and a politics of non-conformity with state and capital. These are values this flyer appeals to. The learning that children will experience at this school is to be 'enlivened by an artistic way of working and a focus on observation to educate the whole human being'. This is education that does not 'espouse merely materialistic values' but aims to form 'young adults who can think, judge and act freely and responsibly' (Anonymous undated, 'Steiner School'). This in turn is a clear vision of an ideal society of persons who are holistic and artistic in their understandings, more spiritual than material, and freethinking.

But though Egan's theory of schools representing aims of society can be useful and expresses a conventional way to think about classrooms, I believe there are problems with it. If schools represent conflicting ideals, then representing more than one becomes a problem. Schools become confused. But if we think of schools as *doing* these values, conflicting as they might be, we become more able to deal with multiplicity without accusing anyone of confusion. We can easily believe in doing one thing and then another. For example, in the Government School advertising, all three of Egan's goals are told as important. Overall, the booklet gives the sense that Government School has created itself as a place so much like a good and happy society that children will naturally become socialised, will learn, and develop as individuals by their time there. What we see is these three goals integrated in such a way as to claim to make the ideal society in the present and for the future.

This point about the 'ideal society' is important. I suggest that Egan's three aims might be logically inconsistent, but even when combined they make sense within particular visions of ideal 'societies'. By identifying a school's aims we can see just how they position themselves within society and what changes they hope to initiate in the social future. This is to say that we should extend Egan's account and render the school-society nexus in terms of how a school represents itself as (re)producing an ideal present and future society. Classrooms are not just a part of society, but are working to remake society. This is evident in the ways schools advertise themselves.

This, I believe, makes an important methodological and ethical difference. In Egan's account, educators and parents seem confused advocates of incoherent positions on what schools should do. By my account, educators and parents educate in ways that are coherent and sensible in order to achieve what they take to be the ideal potential society their children should inhabit. What they represent to parents, carefully and thoughtfully, is a vision where all three of Egan's goals – socialising, knowledge uptake, and individual development – may in various ratios naturally occur together. Some schools emphasise the social, and others the individual, but all give some weight to all three.

So this is one solution to the question 'what is a classroom' – it is a unit within a school that in turn is a unit within a particular vision of society (and aiming to produce or reproduce this vision). A classroom represents and enacts a vision of an ideal future. In each, the classroom researcher is to participate as if within a microcosm of (the ideal) society. They are part of that specific culture. As such, they are to contribute to a complex of behaviours that enact meanings and beliefs. These meanings and beliefs are then to inform their description of these classrooms as ethnographic worlds. They are to represent that classroom fairly and fully. I have suggested that this extends the account of the school-society nexus presented by Egan. But we can give a better account of what a classroom is. It is better not for descriptive purposes, but for developing an ethical sociology of education. I pursue this alternative answer now.

## WHAT IS A CLASSROOM? UNTANGLING THE KNOT OF CLASS

I have said above that a class can be thought of as nesting in a school and in an educational tradition. But nestled within the word 'class' are several other meanings. Class is a broad term referring to social and economic relationships; it is about group membership and identity; also it is about making groups, classifying. These associations are built into the language that we use, and as I will argue here, they are also built into the material life of classrooms.

Here I explore the term 'class' in order to build an ethico-political account of classrooms. To some extent this is a literal-minded approach. It is also animated by a conviction that already in the language we use are metaphors that guide our (re) constituting of our world. Rather than assume that there is some term that lies underneath all classrooms, we should better understand the words that are used in and about classrooms. Instead of searching beyond our sites of enquiry for metaphors to describe those sites, we should talk critically in the language that is used. Remembering that as a noun 'class' denotes socio-economic groups, questions of membership and its denial, and hierarchies of cultural and financial power, allows us to speak of classes of children in particular schools as already marked by these socio-economic distinctions. They already have classed bodies. 'Class' is also a verb. 'To class' is to put into groups, categories, typologies, or hierarchies. Learning to class or classify – to segment the world in particular ways – is one of the key tasks of primary school children. They are learning to have classing bodies.

Hence, one answer to the question 'what is a class?' is that it is a structured group of classed and classing bodies. This is a material answer, but with it comes an ethical consideration for the researcher.

As researchers we also have classed and classing bodies. We attend or work in universities or government agencies. We have particular cultural capital, social status, and relations to governance. These relations class us in complex ways. Moreover, we are adept at making knowledge by grouping or classifying information. We do not pass the government and university ethics committees that regulate classroom research without the necessary signs of these academically classing bodies. But, when we do enter classrooms, we might find ourselves among a class of people we feel uncomfortable with, socially, intellectually, or physically. We might also find that our ability to classify is inappropriate to the classroom, for teachers might act in ways that we have not been taught to classify or been taught to classify unfavourably. We might find that our classed and classing body is challenged in new ways. We have responsibilities to the children and teachers we research, but in these challenges to our own class and classing, we feel threatened, confused, or compromised. Or, equally dangerous to those we intervene with, we might find our judgements of good or bad seem all too self-evident.

I pursue 'class' then as a hinge that joins the socio-material relations in classrooms and the ethico-cognitive responsibility of classroom researchers. I start by telling a story about an interaction with a child rewritten into the language of class relations. This shatters what seemed to be a commonplace moment in the relations between child, peers, and researcher to reveal conflicts between classed and classing bodies. Next I turn to questions of what we do and what we should do with metaphors. I work with Haraway's notion of the heuristic 'knot' (2004). This explains 'class' as useful because its constituent strings lead to the apparently diverse, but in fact closely connected, elements I am interested in. These are the connections between social and material position and the 'right' to know. These are knots that tie up the researcher just as much as the classrooms they research. In the third section I explore some times when my researcher's classed body responds in powerful corporeal ways to the classrooms I visit. Reactions of this kind must have some implications for participant-observation research. This is a moment of reflexive confession. It opens up, however, into more theoretical concerns in the fourth section. Here I explore what happens when ways of classing and being classed clash or interrupt when a researcher enters a classroom. Using Kathryn Addelson's notion of double participation, I ponder the question of how to represent events when they exactly challenge the skills of classifying sanctioned by the university.

## Classed and Classing Bodies

> Mr. Robertson marks the books immediately after the spelling test. Sitting at
> his desk, he calls out that Michael got all fifteen words correct. I'm standing

by the wall, beside two children, a boy and a girl, who have been seated in front of their teacher's desk for the rest of the year. Referring to Michael, the boy says to me, 'he spells like a fifteen-year-old'. His own book is given back. Having read his score he continues, 'I spell like I'm seven years and two months. I'm the worst in the grade'. Like the other children in this room, he is aged nine or ten. He explains further: 'It's because I came from a different school. I've only been here a few months, since the start of the year. It was a really bad school, just a government school' (Author field notes, Independent School, 16 March 2007).*

On my first day in this classroom, this boy named Jayden helps me become aware of the social and material orders that exist here. For him these are visible through the relative talents of the other students. As he talks he places himself in several classes at once. He tells me he is in the class of seven-year-old spellers. He is part of the cohort of his age and grade, but in the position of worst. And he classes himself as (having recently become) part of this school, and thus part of the socio-economic relations that make this a 'good' school. From this new position, he is able to say his old school was bad because it was government funded.

While he makes these relationships real through the words he uses, his relations to the others in the class are also being made through material arrangements. Seated up front with only one other student (instead of in a group of four or six as the rest of the class are arranged), he is set apart. He often turns to speak to the boys behind him, to join in conversations or to try to get help with work. Mostly they ignore him but sometimes talk until the teacher tells Jayden to turn around. His uniform is new, but unlike the other kids he wears it messily, shirt untucked, and hair untidily long. He is perhaps saying 'I know I do not belong (and I don't care)'. Perhaps it is to make up for these distances from his class that he works for my friendship.

To me he boasts. He has seen me arrive on my bicycle, and tells me that he has two bikes. He describes them and tells me their cost as 'one thousand dollars

---

* Throughout this thesis, field notes are not claimed as verbatim records of what was said. In most cases words were written down minutes after I heard them. They do, however, record the sense of what was said.

or something'. He tells me about the number and type of his parents' cars. He tells me how much money he has saved: one thousand five hundred dollars. He plans to buy a motorbike. 'What's the best university in the world?' he asks, and says he will go there. These claims about money and future possibilities, he perceives, are the things that impress those who surround him.

Perhaps they do, but they don't impress me. A government-school educated, middle-class, anti-consumerist feminist, I internally – and sometimes externally – rail against his troubling position of privilege: those cars, this school, that projected future. Over and over at this school I feel resentments welling up inside me that I deal with by thinking patronising thoughts. I am reminded of Bourdieu (see, for example, Bourdieu 1984). These people have economic capital that I, with only cultural capital, sneer at.

I also build interpretations that fix this class as part of the socio-economic system that assigns human value on the basis of owning money and objects. Feeling this system to be unjust, I also feel its reproduction through the institution of this classroom to be unjust. When I find out what the fees are for this place, I am shocked. To be a member of this classroom, one's parents must be members of another class: those who can afford to pay the equivalent of almost my whole yearly earnings for a year of their children's education. Doing so, they must believe, will reap significant rewards, financial and otherwise, for their children. Socio-economic class is to be reproduced, though in ways that are not solely financial. These children are to have musical, sporting, and artistic talents. They are to be good citizens and Christians (Gregory undated). They are to have the skills of self-actualisation (Saulwick and Muller 1999). I read these words with a cynicism that says 'these are the values of the rich'.

But though surrounded at home and at school with the material markers of an exclusive socio-economic class, Jayden does not seem happy. Largely this appears due to his failures to fit, academically or socially, with the rest of his classmates. He is less able than others to perform the cognitive and social acts that will reap positive attention, and he is aware of this. Week after week he does badly in spelling. The words are not chosen at random, however, but because they display a similar phonetic form. The arrangement of English into phonetic groups is mapped on the wall of this classroom in the form of a 'Thrass Chart', a literacy education tool developed by Denyse Richie and Alan Davis.* On it, each phonetic group is put in a box, in an order roughly following the alphabet. Each square contains the letters that make the sound, and the word and picture of an exemplary noun. For example, this week Mr Robertson has chosen words that all contain 'ph', a phonetic grouping illustrated on the chart by 'dolphin'. Jayden, however, is worse than others in his class at recognising the common elements of each word and applying them during the spelling test. Sometimes he puts an 'f', sometimes a 'ph'. What he is failing at is an act of *classification*; seeing that all these words are related by their common phonetic elements.

He also regularly fails to find the right topics of conversation with his class-mates. He tries telling them about his other friends, or about basketball, or about his parents' cars. Sometimes these gambits work, or work for a while, but eventually he is sent back to his desk or returns there after the other children ignore him or are rude. His categories of good topics of conversation and good social behaviours are not quite right. He gets the most positive attention from his classmates when, usually by mistake, he gets in trouble with the teacher. The line between good and bad behaviours that is supposed to govern this class is not yet clear to him. Social classifications are not yet easy for him to enact.

I decide that I like this child, tacitly applying mental tags that read 'sweet, but socially inept, needs to work harder to catch up'. These stay attached to him in my mind and in our interactions, and now I write about him emphasis-ing those features that make him this type of figure. In my telling these tags all relate him to class – to failed bids at class membership, socially with his peers, and physically in where he is seated; to the socio-economic class of his parents who have removed him from a 'bad' (read poor) school and put him here; to his conversational emphasis on his socio-economic class that fit the discourses of this classed school; to his difficulties in making phonetic classes work for him in his spelling test; and to his classing of himself as 'the worst'.

I have also told this as a story of my own class and my own classing. Forming an oppositional stance to the material wealth and consumerist values of this school, I tell others and myself about my own middle-class – my university

---

* See 'Thrass: For Phonetics Teaching and ESL' <http://www.thrass.com.au> [accessed June 2007].

educated, feminist class – my cultural capital. I work this position into my classing of what happens at this school, how I understand and respond to the social
and learning practices that occur in this classroom. Recognising this clumping
of material and analytic problems provides the motivation to explore the power
of the supposedly innocent, but multiply designating, 'class'.

## Class as an Analytic Knot

I want to use 'class' as an analytic device that shows the co-joint and inseparable
nature of the several notions that the term class denotes. It is a word that, to use
Haraway's notion, acts as a knot (Haraway 1994). We can follow its strings out-
wards variously to shared and contested group membership, to socio-economic
differences embedded in the backgrounds and futures of individuals, and to acts
of classifying performed by teacher, children, and researcher. 'Class' lets us look
in several directions at once. Moreover, 'class' is a metaphor that *already* structures the life of the classroom. Classrooms are so permeated by the metaphor
of class that we forget that it is both metaphorically and materially significant
to what classrooms are.

Attending to metaphor can illuminate things previously hidden; just what
appears depends on the metaphor used. There are two main ways that metaphor
has been used in classroom studies. One is to study the language used in and
about classrooms to find their common metaphorical centre. This is the technique advocated by Lakoff and Johnson (1980), and applied to classrooms by,
for example, Hermine Marshall. In 1988 and again in 1990, Marshall critiqued
the use of the metaphors used in classrooms that gathered as 'classroom-as-
workplace', suggesting that it focused attention on task completion and product
creation rather than on learning. Suggesting that 'classroom-as-learning-place'
would better highlight the processes of learning, she worked to encourage
teachers to think and act in ways that encouraged processes instead of products
(Marshall 1988; Marshall 1990). If we were to follow this technique we would
study language to identify common words used in and about classrooms and
study their implications for classroom practice. We would find a metaphor that
seemed to sum these up. Metaphor in this work is a tool for naming animating

values within classrooms. Doing so, however, fails to recall that classrooms are also material places, assembled with people and things that already have political and social lives.

A second way to use metaphor is to search outside the classroom for things to compare the classroom to. Whereas the first technique would search for metaphors *in* classrooms, here we would search for good metaphors *for* classrooms. These will hopefully work to reveal something new about the nature of all classrooms. Working in and for broader analytic concerns, this technique finds suitable metaphors to enhance a particular theoretical approach to classrooms.

This has its dangers, perhaps the most obvious of which is that the metaphors chosen can have practical implications. This is a problem that Keith Sawyer identifies. He shows that the metaphor 'teaching is performance' has crucially mis-modelled the nature of teaching in ways that have been fed back into teacher education. He explains that 'the performance metaphor suggests that an effective actor could be an excellent teacher without even understanding anything' (Sawyer 2004: 12). This had the effect of denigrating the knowledge and skill of teachers and supporting the writing of scripted lessons for them to simply present to the students. Instead of using the 'performance' metaphor, he suggests, we should talk and think of 'teaching as improvisation' (Sawyer 2004). This should serve as a reminder that in applying metaphors from outside of schools we must be very careful that they only describe usefully and do not carry theoretical implications that can be damaging.

Perhaps one way to avoid this danger is to follow Helen Verran in choosing metaphors that seem only to describe, and that are too clunky to slip as if naturally into actual classrooms. This is the approach used by Verran when she talks about classrooms as 'organised/organising micro-worlds'. By this she means 'specific materially arranged times/places where rituals, repeated routine performances, occur' (Verran 2001: 159). This is a useful phrase because it contains within it the joint nature of classrooms as structured and productive. Using this term, however, we miss out on the opportunity language affords to call up the actual and the figurative simultaneously. Because it is designed to disrupt our thinking, it is hard to find actual classrooms in the phrase 'organised/organising micro-worlds'. It is a phrase that could describe almost anything.

Perhaps another solution would be to find metaphors from other scholarly work that are hard to slip into classrooms but that also link us to broader theories. Here, however, it is *description* of the material reality of classrooms that might be compromised. It is tempting, for example, to talk of classrooms in terms that Edwin Hutchins uses in his study of distributed cognition (Hutchins 1995). His work takes place on a naval ship, and indeed the metaphor of the 'ship' works productively to image the process he is interested in. Arguing that we should understand some thinking as going beyond the skin of individuals, he shows how each member of staff on a naval ship is an expert in only parts of the larger routines necessary to sail. The ship succeeds because all staff share conversational routines that powerfully link those routines into one. No one person could know, perform, or control all the routines necessary to bring the ship into port, but through the correct joining of routines the ship is docked.

When applied to classrooms, the ship metaphor does some useful analytic work, highlighting the assembled nature of classrooms, filled as they are with materials and people marked by their lives outside the classroom but for many hours a day isolated together. It makes thinking a group activity, but one that is tightly constrained by relations of authority. The ship metaphor can reveal relations and the power of material objects, but it would also carry dangers because of differences between classrooms and naval ships. Some are to do with authority and expertise. On a naval ship, relations of authority are multi-layered but in a classroom all children are to be subordinated to the teacher. All children are to be roughly equal in expertise, and vastly less experienced and competent than the teacher. It would also misunderstand the aims of classrooms. Taking there to be a clear end point – task completion – that all members of the group share, the ship metaphor makes the work of the classroom into specific, uni-linear, productive processes that would hide the creative, under-determined nature of learning.

Instead of searching for a metaphor used in classrooms or about classrooms, I suggest an approach more like that of Donna Haraway. She explains her work in an interview with Thyrza Goodeve published as the book *How Like a Leaf*. When asked about her use of metaphors from biology, she explains that for her using the language of biology is to highlight simultaneously the literary and literal nature of biology. 'I want to call attention to the simultaneity of fact and fiction, materiality and semioticity, object and trope' (Haraway 2000: 82–83). Hers is an approach that calls us to remember that language and material arrive together.

For Haraway, as for other feminists, the goal of scholarship should not be to describe from a fictional 'outside' but to admit our positions within. This is a better way to produce objective knowledge than the pretence of seeing and speaking from nowhere. Maximally objective knowledge is possible only when researchers are critically situated within their objects of study. We share language with those we study, carrying notions taken so much for granted that we fail to notice them or their implications. This implicates the researcher too, reminding us again of the need to be reflexive about how we fit and what we wish to see. As Sandra Harding wrote to advance the claims to objectivity of standpoint episte- mology, 'objectivism impoverishes its attempts at maximising objectivity when it turns away from the task of critically identifying all of those broad, historical social desires, interests, and values that have shaped the agendas, contents and results' (Harding 2004: 136). The desires, interests, and values come already packaged in our language – that of researchers and participants alike.

Next I explore further this nexus between researcher, language, and situated- ness in classed and classing bodies. What does it mean for doing objective research in classrooms if we are honest about the desires, interests, and values that we carry in our classed and classing bodies?

## Ethics and the Researcher's Classed and Classing Body

At my first meeting to arrange research work at Steiner School, I wear what I consider my most 'hippy' skirt. This is a joke made into a material reality. In clothing my body in this way I am announcing my allegiance to and requesting membership in what I assume is the social and political class of Steiner teach- ers. I am classing them as racially white, politically anti-capitalist, and socio- economically middle-class – hippies. I am showing myself as classed likewise. Certainly, this has some effect on how I am treated; they seem to like me.

My classed and classing body does more than dress up, it feels. After days in the classroom of a government school with a teacher who carefully brings ethics of multiculturalism and mutual responsibility into her teaching, I cycle home feeling deeply happy. Her practice of politics, I feel, touches my heart. Mawkish as this is, it is also sign that her practices of producing relationships between her children and their world gel with my beliefs and aspirations of what schools should do. Her practices meet my expectations as the child of a liberal university education and of the political and social views I have been embedded in. This subject position is again intrinsically part of my classed and classing body, a body that feels as part of its thinking.

Such feelings are not always positive matters of simple connection with others who seem to occupy the same group as oneself. Meeting parents during my time at the special school for low-IQ students, I experience a sense of confused and cruel ambivalence. Many of these parents are evidently low in financial and intellectual capital. They lack teeth, are obese, or wear strange and dirty clothes. I am witnessing the reproduction, literally, of society's most marginal class. At times I feel this as disgust, a fear of bodies so unlike my own, bodies profoundly marked by their positions in hierarchies of intelligence (and discourses of genetics) and socio-economic status. At other times I experience these moments as guilt for classing and judging others in such terms. This is brought into relief when I meet Roderick's mum. He was suffering an epileptic seizure and she has come to take him to the doctor. A well-dressed woman who left work in her SUV, she talks to me about her son's disability. I feel a deep sympathy, accompanied by shock that I have not experienced such feelings with any other parent. She is like me, in ways the other parents I have met are not. And now I can see that my own social-intellectual class is affecting my classing of them.

The unfamiliarity of the ways of living and thinking in these classrooms is surprising and invigorating. Places of differently classed bodies are also places of different practices of classifying. This is especially the case in the most differently socially situated of classrooms, that of this Special School. What its teachers, Diane and Michaela, practise with great skill is not delivering planned lessons but responding appropriately to the rapidly shifting needs of students. They are enacting the feminist vision of the knower who does not look and think from afar, but is flexible, responsive, and responsible. They are doing a relational metaphysics. My habit of forming classes about the 'real' via mental reflection are challenged by their practices. Their classification of good knowing gels with what I intellectually agree with, but have never formally learnt to practise.

The challenge I face in appropriately analysing these practices of classifying that are so radically different from my own is one of ethics. The question is how to use my classed and classing body in ways that will give due credit to such differently classed and classing bodies. This is the problem of double participation.

## Double Participation

> Before the kids are allowed into the bag room to collect their lunch, Diane goes in to check it's clean. Standing by the door, she announces, 'There's no food on the floor there now, and there won't be any after lunch either, will there? Sometimes,' she continues, 'food mysteriously appears there on the floor, but I'm sure it won't today'. Dwayne suggests, excited, that maybe there is a ghost, but Diane says, clear and firm, 'No. There is no ghost'. The kids get seated with their sandwiches, and Diane turns to me. 'You'll go back to your university and say "Geez! They were the stupidest people I ever spent a day with"'. (Author field notes, Special School, 8 October 2007).

Diane is pointing out to me the double-ness of my participation. I am here in this classroom, watching and joining in with what happens. But, she is suggesting, I don't really fit here. I will return to university and say 'geez, how stupid they were' to the people I really belong with, roll my eyes and criticise, or mock those I have been researching.

Though, in fact, I was always impressed by what I saw at Special School, Diane's prediction mapped a general problem in the ethics of fieldwork. Kathryn Addelson refers to this problem as 'double participation'. Describing the research done by Prudence Rains towards writing her 1971 book *Becoming an Unwed Mother: A Sociological Account,* Addelson points out that Rains was part of two types of collective action. She was part of the 'ongoing personal and everyday collective lives of the subjects'. Simultaneously 'there was the collective activity that she took part in as a professional researcher, activity that constituted her discipline and the institutions of science'. (Addelson 1994: 160). Her participation was double because she was acting in and for two separate groups – unwed mothers and sociologists. She was engaged in 'double participation'.

What Diane was pointing out was that I too was engaged in 'double participation' between her classroom and my university. This was partly a matter of differently classed bodies. In her version I would return from this low-income city margin to my university in the CBD. There I would sit with friends and colleagues rich in cultural, if not financial capital, and find ways to act – to speak and write – with them. She was reminding me that my body was not embedded in the same hierarchies of wealth, knowledge, or status as those bodies I was acting with in her classroom.

Further, she was suggesting that I would classify what I was experiencing in terms my university colleagues would already agree with: that the collective action at a school for low-IQ students was itself stupid. My classed body, she was saying, opened onto a classing body. Again her prediction was insightful. Universities are sites rich in rules for how to classify information. My classifying habits are built by participation in university knowledge practices, particularly those of the disciplines I have specialised in. Each discipline has rules that guide how to chunk up the world into segments. These rules are shared (to some extent) across a university system, constituting standards – a 'set of agreed-upon rules for the production of (textual and material) objects' (Bowker and Star 1999: 13). These provide cognitive authority, placing us, 'in the *local* sites of laboratory and field [and classroom], not as participants but as "judging observers" who are themselves to be unjudged' (Addelson 1994: 161). Only by showing myself capable of certain classing actions could I have attained my position as PhD student. Over years of writing essays and sitting exams, I had passed through gates kept closed except to those who could write in ways that showed an ability to put ideas in groups in a particular way. And it was by being a PhD student that I had gained the ethics clearances and agreements from principals necessary to being allowed here. From success in approved systems of classifying comes access to sites for classifying.

Diane's classroom did not work on skills of thoughtful and rational classification like those practised in universities, but on quick, flexible responses to flows of action. These were ways of acting that I found myself unused to, feeling bodily and mentally clumsy much of the time. In contrast to those of Diane and her fellow teachers, my skills at classifying were unsuited to this classroom context. A test came one day when Diane was away and we had a relief teacher new to this type of school. Before lunch he sat and read from a book of fables the class was already familiar with. This should have been easy; Michaela, the teacher aide, assured us that the class loved this book. He read the first story right through, including the closing moral. 'Any questions?' he asked. A couple of kids described parts of the story. He turned to the next story. I could see that his lesson was not working, and I thought that his problem was that he was not helping the children build groups of situations when these morals might apply. I believed I could solve his problem by pushing children into making classes of situations that fit the moral of the stories. When the teacher had read the next story right through to the end ('don't throw stones if you live in a glass house'), I suggested we come up with other examples of things that happen at this school to illustrate the moral. I described one: 'if I yelled at everyone else to stop yelling'. The kids responded, but by talking about how you lose a star if you yell. They did not follow me in classifying their lives in terms of these morals, and instead followed a classifying pattern that places actions mentioned in terms of school rules. Both relief teacher and I had failed to form these stories into shapes that the class could respond to in meaningful ways. What this means is that we had failed to reproduce Diane's ways of guiding children's classifications or to create new ones the children would engage with. With Diane they love this book; with us they do not understand.

Recognising that different ways of classifying information are necessary to be a successful part of the action that occurs in Diane's classroom provoked an ethical challenge. It is a challenge I faced not only in the classroom, for through participation there I worked at and gradually improved my skills at responding to children in ways that seemed to work. The bigger ethical challenge came from returning to an academic institution and seeking to describe and explain just why the collective action I had witnessed in Diane's classroom had been so impressive. How to explain the broad value of a way of acting with lowly classed and poorly classifying bodies, to people of high status sourced from their ability to classify in wholly different ways? How to do justice to the talent of Diane and

Michaela, two highly skilled professionals from the margins of their profession? This is a question of how to suitably express the value of a relational metaphysics to a group generally attached to a foundational metaphysics. My solution has been to make these two logics explicit and to be reflexive about my attempts to follow that of relations. My reflexivity is intended to relate my classed and classing body to how I am able to understand classrooms.

## CONCLUSION

I have explored here two modes of ordering that tell us something of what classrooms are. In the first, a mode of ordering based on the relations between school and society, we were able to think about educational traditions and goals for individual and social futures. We saw schools presenting themselves as environments for the production of people suited to (making) ideal societies. Here we also saw the participant-observation researcher as having the ethical duty to represent these classrooms in terms of the school's meanings and values.

In the second mode we explored the classroom as an assemblage of classed and classing bodies. Here was the double-ness of being materially and socially positioned *and* expected to classify in particular ways: to be classed and classing. This seems to me to be both a more useful and a more ethical account. These experiences in classrooms forced my classed and classifying body into acting with the very different classed and classifying bodies of others.

For your author, knowing comes through participation in and for two collectivities (classroom and university) both of different classes and with different modes of classifying. This could be emotionally and psychologically difficult. I was occupying a 'borderland': Bowker and Star's term for the situation of having 'two communities of practice co-exist[ing] in one person' (Bowker and Star 1999: 304). This, I would suggest, is always part of doing participant-observation in some way or another and it is a rich place from which to generate understanding. It impacts on how we are able to represent classrooms in writing, for being a classed and classing body myself I cannot simply tell 'how it was'. What I tell instead is how I was able to understand by following out the knotted strings of 'class'.

**2**

# DEFINING IMAGINATION IN PRACTICE

WHEN I TELL PEOPLE WHAT I AM WRITING, A COMMON REACTION IS TO ASK 'how are you defining imagination?' For a long time I would acknowledge, sighing, that, yes, this is a problem. Why a problem? Because imagination is a word that so evidently means many things at the same time.

My questioners captured this truth. Children also expressed it. Here is a nine-year-old, writing on the topic 'a time you used your imagination'. For the sake of clarity, I have corrected his spelling and punctuation.

> I use my imagination when I play sport. I imagine that there's a big crowd cheering for me. I use my imagination when I write stories. I use my imagination when I play the PlayStation. I use my imagination when I read chapter books. I use my imagination when I'm playing games like shooting. I use my imagination when I am having a break (Catholic School, writing piece: 0, 4).

So, defining imagination seems to be a problem because it is many things, or many processes, or has many functions. Many books about imagination start by pointing out the multiplicity or complexity of the term. Commonly the authors then use one of two strategies to deal with the problem. Sometimes they argue that there is one thing that we really (should) mean by imagination (Sartre 1948; Sartre 1962; Williams 1991; Currie and Ravenscroft 2002). This might take the form of a typology classifying the several things that imagination really means (see, for example, McGinn 2004). Alternatively, they posit some essential set of properties that diverse forms of imagination share. To Greene, for example, the assorted forms of imagination are all 'visions of what should be' (Greene 1995: 5). For Vygotsky, all imagination is the second and more important of the two types of human thought, reproductive and combinatorial, or creative activity (Vygotsky 2004: 9). In either strategy, the 'problem' of multiplicity is dissolved in favour of singularity.

My strategy here will be quite different: I will suggest that a word having multiple meanings is only a problem if you take a particular view of what meaning is. My argument is essentially an updated version of the later Wittgenstein, and owes much to Paul Lieberman's 'Imagination: Looking in the Right Place (and in the Right Way)' (Lieberman 2003; see also Diamond 1991). Again, this is an attempt to move away from representation and towards practice. After describing this view of meaning, I will work to provide in more detail the assorted modes in which teachers define imagination – as intrinsic way of being, as skill that is enjoyed by some, as intentional or unintentional practice, and as useful strategy. Finally, I will propose a tactic necessary to deal with this particular range of definitions. What we need to do, I will suggest, is engage with the practices that our teachers use in their classrooms and which they have conglomerated for us in their words.

## WHAT IS MEANING?

### *External Reference?*

As Lieberman, a clinical psychotherapist, observes, 'we tend to have the following idea about the meanings of words: there are objects, call them meanings, that are what the word refers to' (Lieberman 2003: 21). This is a view that sees meaning as referring to some object or process 'out there'. It is sometimes referred to as the correspondence theory of truth. This type of meaning is commonly associated (ontologically) with realism, (epistemologically) with a Cartesian divide of subject and world, (methodologically) with empiricism and analytic philosophy.

In this tradition we would say that there is some specific meaning, some object or process, which we refer to when we say 'imagination'. Multiplicity would be difficult to deal with. It would suggest that there are several things out there that are covered by the word 'imagination' and that for clarity we should decide which one is imagination and which we should use other words for (like empathy, creativity, and so on). We would be pushed towards asking 'but what do we really mean?'

## Convention?

Since Wittgenstein's (1953) *Philosophical Investigations,* and as an outflow of more sophisticated and sympathetic accounts of the linguistic and social lives of the earth's people, we are less likely to state that meaning is a matter of external reference. Instead, we are likely to conceive of meaning as being like a web, as in Sassure's *Langue,* or, in Wittgenstein's famous term, as part of a 'language game'. In this view meaning happens as we use language as a matter of social convention and negotiation. This understanding of meaning has been useful to theories of social constructivism and of relativism, and is used in textual analysis (it is used, for example, by Walkerdine (1988) in her analysis of children's understanding of mathematical reasoning).

In this tradition we would analyse what people say about imagination, asking questions like 'what do they compare it to? What metaphors do they use?' and 'What is not imagination?' We would ask of our speakers' words, what do *they* really mean? What does this tell us about the net of meanings in which imagination is caught? This again implies that there is some underlying object or process that speakers refer to, albeit a potentially different object for each speaker. So while this strategy deals better with multiplicity, it does so by positing speakers as referring to their own views of a distant object. In this picture, language works on the assumption that others mean something close to what we ourselves mean.

## Conglomerated Practice?

Lieberman suggests that the version of the language game that I have described above, and that has exerted so much influence, is a misreading of Wittgenstein.

It is to miss the philosophy. We should look also, Lieberman says, at how we *use* language as part of our embodied lives. He gives the example of stating the time: 'it is three o'clock'. This should not be read as an assertion of the essential three-ness of the hour or as a representation of a fact about the sun's location in the sky. Nor, however, should it be read as just a socially conventional statement we could make at the moment its meaning has been agreed on (and is kept in clocks and watches). It is the case that when we say 'it is three o'clock' we refer to a social agreement about the sun's location in the sky as well as an agreement about how to index that as 3pm. But this is not all we mean. Instead, we should look at the whole web of practices, with and without objects, which are pulled together when we say that it is three o'clock. These include, and are not limited to, practices with clocks, watches and mobile phones, working days, school days and weekends, practices of starting and ending activities, the arrangement of mealtimes, the measurement of ages, and so on. Lieberman defends this move by suggesting that, apart from being what Wittgenstein intended, it is also obvious. 'What we gain by giving up [external referentiality] is a new attention to what is already before our eyes but which, it seems, we tend to ignore: our verbal and nonverbal practices, forms of life, language games' (Lieberman 2003: 22).

This may or may not be an accurate reading of Wittgenstein's work (what he really meant), but it is useful here for it illuminates in terms of meaning what scholars like Verran suggest: namely that we study the relatedness of subjects and objects in practice. It encourages us to think both about how people use words and how they do what they are talking about. It is about words as part of, not just descriptions of, what our world is. Words, this is to say, are tools that help us conglomerate our practices and are part of our practices.

We can use people's words to help us develop sensitivity to their practices, their modes of doing imagination. Asking teachers what imagination means is a way of asking them to conglomerate for us the 'imagination' they practise. Their answers will make us better placed to notice what they do in their classrooms with words (especially 'imagine' and 'imagination'), with books and pens and paper, with counting blocks and numerals, with arguing children. Only by spending time with them in classrooms, as we do in part two of this book, will we learn how they actually do practise imagination.

## WHAT DO YOU THINK OF WHEN I SAY 'IMAGINATION'?

Listen with me to what teachers say imagination means. I have asked, as the very first question in an interview, 'what do you think of when I say imagination?' This question is purposefully open. And it elicits answers that show imagination as perhaps a state, perhaps a thing or perhaps a process. It will help us understand what they believe makes a good teacher, and what they take to be the educational task. It will also tell us what they think children are naturally like and what they want for the children in their classrooms to be able to do and be when they grow up. It will tell us about how each teacher connects good imagining and good living.

What teachers' answers reveal are options for thinking about what imagination is as we shift our notions of what human agents are. Put another way, each teacher tells us something different about what type of thing imagination can be. These senses of what is possible and what is important are a guide and a constraint on their practice. These different imaginations assume and reproduce different types of human-ness, or more specifically, child-ness. We hear from two teachers about imagination as an attribute of persons. They disagree however about whether it is a state of being or a talent. Is it something we are or that we have?

This is a possible division used by Edwin Hersh. He suggests that we understand imagination either as 'describing a particular *domain* or zone of our experience characterised primarily as one of unreality, fiction, and falsehood, or, alternatively, as an essential *dimension* of our being, namely an essential aspect inherent to all of human reality' (Hersch 2003: 57, emphasis in original). Aligning these two positions with analytic and continental philosophy respectively, Hersh is formalising the divide between imagination as something we have (a domain of unreality, fiction, or falsehood clearly bounded from reality) or something we are (an aspect or dimension of ourselves and our human reality).

Other teachers divide the possibilities differently. They say imagination is both something that we are and that we have, just as we both are and have bodies (Merleau-Ponty 2004; Mol and Law 2007). It is not appropriate to isolate imagination as either a domain or a dimension. These two teachers talk of imagination as something that we *do*, and their answers are divided by the degree of agency involved. These teachers disagree on whether we do imagination or have it done in us. Do we purposefully imagine or is it elicited by the sensual world around us?

There is a final possibility: that imagination is something we do for particular strategic purposes. This retains the sense of imagination as practice and sidesteps the problem of agency. Whether we consciously choose to imagine something is less relevant than the purpose it serves in our conscious and unconscious lives. Our imaginations can do fantasy and thinking, solve psychic and cognitive problems, give us pleasure and understanding.

From our five teachers' versions of what imagination is we can also infer important things about their sense of, and practices with, children. How teachers talk about imagination is based on assumptions, shared to some extent throughout the school, about what children are. These are basic to the behaviours expected from children and permitted in schools – through rules, suggestions, tasks, materials supplied in playgrounds and classrooms, divisions of time, and so on.

How teachers talk about imagination, and the children they figuratively and materially produce, is our starting point.

## Children are… Naturally Imagining

> ME: What do you think of when I say 'imagination'?
> SHIRLEY: We forget that children […] [imagination]'s just like their natural state, we forget that that's what they need, time to live in that. Young children, I've learnt to watch them, and you find, and I've found that when you talk to them about anything, and if we learn to talk in pictures, you can see them building what they're hearing, and it kind of happens in front and above, and you can see them actually building that, and so […] it's something that we're born with, it's inherent (Steiner School, author interview with teacher, 15 June 2007).

What Shirley is telling us is that imagining is what and where children are. Imagination is not simply something that some children have while others don't, nor is it something children can choose to do or not. Rather imagination is part of the definition of what makes a child a child, and what makes a child able to grow up into a good (normal, natural) adult. Imagination is a child's 'natural state', something they need to be in, something they need to be, as a part of being a child. Here we have a description that identifies imagination and child-ness as co-determining states of being. Children *are* imagining.

This way of talking about imagination is part of a wider way of talking about children. Throughout the interview, we can sense a particular type of child – interestingly, a child much like Shirley describes herself as having been.

Shirley sees the child as having a deep need, a hunger for stories that they can imagine with. This child is threatened severely by the adult world; at stake is their capacity to think and to be good. Their minds and their morals are threatened by the horrors that abound in the adult world in its billboards, its noise, its six o'clock news. If allowed to live in imagination, children will naturally develop an intellectual life and the pictures they have in their minds will fade. But until that time, this child is guarded as she builds a little world, thinking in pictures during the whole of their school day. She might be dreamy just as Shirley claims she was as a child. She might be a pain in the neck, as Shirley jokes she was. But certainly she is happy, balanced, and enlivened. She will gradually grow into a responsible adult.

Children who do not get enough opportunity to occupy their imagination will be lacking a basic nutrient necessary for their normal development. Just as babies need their mother's milk, so children need to imagine through stories. Talking about the reaction of children at mainstream schools to being told a story from their teacher's mind, Shirley says:

> There's something in them that cries, that sucks it up like a sponge, sucks it out of you, they are desperate for it, even though it would be difficult for them to identify it since they've never had it, but when they get it and it's the first time they're experienced that, never have I seen anyone go, 'Jesus, just go and get the book' (Steiner School, author interview with teacher, 15 June 2007).

## Children are... Naturally Variable

> ME: What do you think of when I say 'imagination'?
>
> MR ROBERTSON: 'Ummm [...] the things you think of, the word pictures in your mind, or the pictures in your mind, ah, imagining something that isn't there at the moment, ability to construct in your mind ideas about things [...] that sort of thing. Imagination. Some children don't have it. Some children, when we are doing creative writing, find it very difficult, they are very literal. I quite like imagination. I think it's very good to imagine something that could be, good skill. There you go, that'll do (Independent School, author interview with teacher, 17 April 2007).

Mr Robertson has given an answer that says imagination is a thing to have: it is a specific skill or talent, an ability that some children have and others don't. It is a good and useful skill, but its lack is not disabling except during certain tasks, like creative writing. For Mr Robertson, imagination is something individuals do or do not have.

In Mr Robertson's words, imagination is made as one attribute in the collection that children are born with. Instead of being a natural state that all children should live in, as we see in Shirley's answer, imagination is a skill.

This notion blends with images of children as described throughout the interview. In this interview, Mr Robertson's conjures up two imagining children. One is fading to the point of vanishing. This child is only six or seven years old and is lying on the mat, eyes closed, as the teacher tells them a story. They are flying on a magic carpet. This says that the skill of imagination is used less as children go through school. The other child, aged nine or ten as grade four children are, is sitting up at a desk, listening to the teacher as he reminds them of past lessons, and builds up into new lessons, using words that have pictures attached. This child is an 'imagineer'. She is visualising, making plans, and writing lists. This child is conceiving their assignments in topic work, and is taking on a persona in drama. They are not feeling inferior. They are thinking what it would be like if they could run harder or be first. But not all children are doing this, and it is not a problem. These other children are literal and, apart from having trouble with creative writing, are just as intelligent and as capable as their peers (Independent School, author interview with teacher, 17 April 2007).

## Children do Imagination... by Intentionally Opening their Minds

> ME: What do you think of when I say 'imagination'?
>
> JUSTINE: Ummm – I think of opening your mind up to other possibilities and seeing things differently, umm, just drawing on ideas and experiences, imagining putting yourself into a different time a different space, to think a little, umm, outside the square, to let, I guess, to open up your mind to things that are more creative, and, yeah, to let images and ideas flow through your mind (Government School, author interview with teacher, 29 May 2007).

Justine describes imagination as something that we do when we open our minds. Imagination is something that we can *do*, but crucially we do it in order to find a different perspective. This is why we must allow and encourage children to do imagination: to make sure they will have a sense of empathy and creativity in their lives. Imagination is something we do as a matter of choice, that we do when we choose to open our minds. It is directed and useful action.

What type of child does Justine see alongside this notion of imagination? He or she is playing mothers and fathers, learning roles and how to relate to others and to orient themselves in their lessons. This is the modern child that Justine is trying to help her students be. But their game is at risk of coming to a premature end. They feel pressure from adults to get serious, to get to their music lesson or sports training, to forget those childish things, to grow up.

There is also the spectre of another child here, one who is profoundly disabled. Never wondering, never curious, just taking things to be as they are rather than having a sense they could change them. This is the child that Justine perceives herself to have been. She has only recently recognised this in her past because of the disability she believes it gave her. This recognition has occurred since her husband died, and she found herself afloat in a world that she hadn't dreamt of but had to find ways to climb out of. She couldn't do so until she could imagine new futures that would require her own power and agency to build.

Looking back at her young life, she now wishes that someone had encouraged her to imagine then, had taught her of the power of imagination to help us make things anew. Seeing the children around her, their need for free imaginative play to make them flexible agents, she believes they must be protected from adult pressures. They must be encouraged to choose to open their minds (Government School, author interview with teacher, 29 May 2007).

## Children do Imagination... but Need to be Kept in the Real

> ME: What do you think of when I say 'imagination'?
>
> DIANE: I think of what happens in people's heads that they don't, that doesn't necessarily mean that it's connected with anything real or not, it's just where their heads go. At different times. Things that evoke imagination, you know, smells from the past, things from the past, things that you want to do. So it's sort of forward and back (Special School, author interview with teacher, 26 October 2007).

For Diane imagination is something that we do, but is not purposeful and not necessarily real. Instead, imagination is evoked by the world around us; its smells, its things that remind us of the past. It is drawn on by undisciplined remembering and desiring bodies. We do not control our relationships with our imaginations even while we engage with it. In doing imagination we are pulled into connections with things real and unreal. What we do when we do imagining is unruly; it is undirected action.

Diane faces the pathological imagination every day. For her, what is and is not 'normal' imagination is a concern. There is only a faint spectre in her interview of the 'normally' imagining child. The normal child is able to distinguish real from unreal. This imagining child feels safe. She is happy pottering alone, in his or her own company, or is happily playing a made up game with a friend – making up their own names and their own countries rather than getting them from TV and movies. This child can empathise; this child can plan and cope with situations.

But, Diane says, many of the children at her school cannot behave like this child because they need the concrete and the here-and-now to transfer things from. They lack the experiences, or the memory of experiences, on which to base elaborated imaginary lives. They are children who have a hole where they should have experiences to supply them with things to imagine from, like pictures of snowy mountains that don't come from TV. They are scared of making their own decisions, overcompensated for their lacks, or frightened of punishment. The teacher responds to their needs, moment by moment, here and now. She doesn't get carried away with the words as if the words were a big deal. Instead she teaches life skills and keeps the children happy and feeling safe. She sticks to the concrete with the children, but needs to be imaginative herself. She imagines, she poses questions, makes plans, and enjoys things. Diane is laughing now, telling me that she's imagining what she will look like in a dress knowing well that she won't look anything like so good (Special School, author interview with teacher, 26 October 2007).

### Children can Use… Multiple Imaginations

ME: What do you think of when I say 'imagination'?

MRS RICH: The things that I think of is, like, thinking creatively, images in your mind, just forming ideas in my mind. That's what I think of. One aspect, I think, [of] imagination is creating things that are totally imaginative and don't really exist. And another part is thinking, no, it's just a form of thinking. Imagine you were there, imagine. So I think of imagination as being fantasy and imagination as being, […] being real. So there's two aspects of imagination that I think of. And both of them valuable for different things. […] I think it's more a thinking tool (Catholic School, author interview with teacher, 11 September 2007).

Here Mrs Rich tells imagination as one of the tools we have in an arsenal of thinking. We might think in fantasy – and then one type of imagination is valuable. We might think about some other time or place – and then 'imagining if' will be valuable. It is a multiple tool applicable in different situations. We do various types of thinking and imagination might help us.

The imagining children told of in Mrs Rich's interview are multiple and marked by their variety. The child has changed over time. Once she was passive, happily sitting at the desk with a book. Now all these multiple children need to be motivated and the teacher is working to give them all reasons to and ways to learn. There are two types of imagining children now in her classroom. One is letting themselves go wherever their imagination takes them, creating crazy and wild things. The other is the child who is using it as a thinking tool. This child is drawing connections in their mind and letting them show, so that the teacher might see how they think. They are advantaged in their ability to learn, to read, to understand things. They are also advantaged in their humanity, able to empathise and build relationships. Each child is different, has slightly different thinking tools, and the teacher must have many strategies ready at all times. The good teacher makes children think always, with open-ended questions that all can answer according to their ability. She makes things fun and boosts esteem. She can do this because she can imagine what her students' home lives might be like. She is always on the ball.

There is also a not-imagining child. This child has trouble expressing themselves and their understanding is weak, though how much is due to intellect and how much with language we can't know. This child needs their teacher to talk of the familiar. To do imagination for Mrs Rich is integral to being a thinking person, whatever one's thought is about (Catholic School, author interview with teacher, 11 September 2007).

## CONCLUSION

Here I have argued that imagination should not be taken to mean any single thing. Rather, I have shown that teachers use it to refer to their various sets of practices in the classroom and with the children they have spent time with over their lives. 'Imagination', I have said, does not represent, but conglomerates practices and possibilities.

This said, the word 'imagination' could not be used to point to just any practices. For language to work, there must be some overlaps between what speakers mean. 'Imagination' could be thought of as what Star and Griesemer (1989) call a 'boundary object'. These are tools – words, rulers, maps, rules, people – that act as interfaces between communities of practice. They are things flexible enough to be adapted to particular needs and yet robust enough to maintain a common identity across boundaries. They are things that can be used differently, and hence mean different things, but still retain enough of their identity to stay together. 'They have different meanings in different social worlds, but their structure is common enough to more than one world to make them recognizable' (Star and Griesemer 1989: 393).

We have seen that, for each of these teachers, imagination conglomerates differently. This does not depend only on the type of school they teach in, but is contingent on their specific circumstances. As we have seen, these circumstances might be related to a teacher's memory of their own childhood, what their students are like, and the materials available to them, the professional development leader who comes to their school, or their school's ways of marketing itself.

What is also evident is that for each teacher, what imagination turns out to be is related to their understandings of what children and humans more generally are like; what the world is like, and how therefore children should best know and imagine. Put another way, these answers to 'what do you think of when I say imagination?' tell us about multiple understandings of good knowing and good living. For Shirley, good knowing is related to our stage of life. Knowers should be protected from tired concepts for as long as they can in order to live well in original and personally relevant ways. For Mr Robertson, good knowing has something to do with knowing our attributes and knowing which realms will allow us to reveal them. Good living is about being able to apply the particular set of skills you have. For Justine, good knowing is being open to possibilities of being other than we are. This makes good living possible for each of us even as our circumstances change, making us able to change who we are and what we do. For Diane, good knowing is about knowing where you are, whether you are connected to the real, the fantastical, to this person, or that thing. Good living has something to do with being happily in touch with whatever, whoever, and wherever – either real or made up, you find yourself. For Mrs Rich, good knowing is flexible and responsive to what we need to do. Good living means always being on the ball to work out what needs to be done, or thought, or connected to now.

# 3

# IMAGINATION AND THEORY BUILDING

Having spent months, on and off, observing and participating in the lives of primary school classrooms, I returned to my desk in a small post-graduate office. I'd been looking forward to this: after months of feeling like all I could do was respond to the onward rush of words and bodies as children and teachers managed the arrival, sitting, standing, talking, writing, playing, telling, and telling-off that makes up a school day, now, *now*, I was going to be able to think. And to help me think, I had the field notes, interviews, pictures, and stories created by children, teachers, and me. I was going to find something in all that to write about.

It was an immediately intimidating proposition. Ten thousand words of notes, over one hundred pictures and the same number of stories, three and a half hours of interviews, and more. Well, I thought, nothing will happen if I just sit here; I should *do* something.

Remembering advice given in the qualitative research methods texts I had studied as an undergraduate, I made a set of file cards. Onto each, I stuck a picture drawn by a child in response to the task 'a time you used your imagination.'

I then set about trying to make sense of these pictures, looking carefully and laying them out in piles and rows on my desk, and sometimes on my floor. In doing so, I was making patterns of similarity and difference. I was using these cards to transform a set of pictures drawn by a hundred different children, some of whom shared a classroom and others who would never meet, into categories of imagination that made sense in and as theories. I was hoping that through my actions the correct theory of what imagination is would emerge.

In fact it was theories – plural – that emerged. I could pile these cards in many ways, all of which made sense in terms of previous theoretical positions and that seemed accurate in terms of classroom life. I noticed this as first one, then another, way of piling the cards made me feel discomforted. I did not wish to endorse some of these ways of piling nor the theories that they implied. I made one theory, then another.

IN THIS CHAPTER I HOPE TO MAKE THE CASE FOR FOUR INTERLINKED CONtentions. My first contention is the easiest. It is that the researcher's imagination is always, to some extent, a bodily imagination. This is to remember that humans are not minds floating above the world, but are inextricably involved in it with flesh and fingers. Doing data analysis by physically moving around concrete objects made this particularly obvious. But if we think of the other forms of work we do while analysing information – for me a matter of drawing mind maps, listing ideas complete with arrows and cross-outs, typing and rearranging with the cut and paste function – we begin to see that all the work we do before a piece of work seems finished is likewise bodily. We do not, or only rarely, find a way to imagine the connection between this piece of information and that piece, without at some stage interacting in a bodily way with the stuff of the world.

So this is contention number one: the imagination necessary to make any claims about new information is done with the help of our bodies. This opens us to a second contention, again made obvious by the concreteness of this particular data set. If the researcher's imagination is bodily then there are multiple possibilities for how they might analyse their data. This means there are multiple theories they can make that will give order and shape to their information. I will soon explore this idea more with the help of Annemarie Mol, John Law, and Kieran Egan. These scholars' work illuminates why multiplicity occurs and gives us good reason to believe that it is not, in itself, a problem. Instead is it is a natural consequence of our general embodied relationships with the world.

Their work does something else too. It is based on the idea that intervention should be the goal of scholarship, not just representation. We are inevitably

intervening so we'd better be careful how. This brings us to my third contention: the problem with the ways I find to pile my data is not that they are bad
representations of the world or of what goes on in the world. In fact, each seems
correct in certain ways and is used to structure school life. However, each carries
with it implications that are distasteful to me for ethical reasons. Each makes me
discomforted when I think of what this would mean for particular children if
applied back into classrooms as the single truth. So the problem with each way
of piling my data is that as theories they would be bad interventions. They are
embedded in, and would further embed in schools, a worrying politics. I will
discuss this contention in the third, and biggest, section of this chapter through
a discussion of three ways to pile my data.

This brings us to my fourth and final contention. I argue, with Helen Verran
and Andrew Pickering, as well as Law and Mol, that we need a different type of
politics to think better about data analysis. In this final section of the chapter I
will introduce a way to frame this new politics funnelled through a final way I
found to pile my data.

## JUSTIFYING MULTIPLICITY

I will start with my second contention that there are multiple ways to theorise
a data set, hoping that my first will be reinforced throughout. In this section,
I provide three ways of understanding the multiplicity of theories. One, Mol's
account, finds multiplicity in the fact of our enactment of reality. With this I
defend multiplicity as being part of how we live. The second, Law's, finds multiplicity in our ways of understanding and communicating about the world. I
use this to explain where my particular stories about imagination come from.
The third, Egan's, I use to hint at the possibility that we will face the problem of
multiplicity more often as time goes on.

### Justifying Multiplicity One: A Consequence of Practice

Let us go further into why my practice of methodological imagination (my
ways of imagining as I did research, analysis, and writing) might have been

generating these multiple accounts. What was happening and should I be alarmed?

The work of Annemarie Mol helps us to see one way into this problem. In her book, *The Body Multiple* (2002), she looks at the practices that make atherosclerosis differently in different parts of one Dutch hospital. She saw patients with the same disease and suffering in various ways being sent to different parts of the hospital for diagnosis and treatment. How their diseased legs and their suffering were dealt with depended on whether they were looked at by the eyes of the walking therapist, the X-rays of clinicians, or the microscopes of pathologists. With the staff's various embodied and technologically enhanced visions for seeing legs, cells, blood vessels, and their tools for treating these – walking therapy, cutting, medication – they made different atheroscleroses. They saw, understood and treated different diseases although all 'really' were atherosclerosis.

In essence, Mol's argument is that because we enact or practise reality (of diseased bodies in her case) we can and do enact it differently in different times and places. This is crucially not an argument about perspectives – that people see or understand the world differently. Rather, she says that we are able to enact things differently *and* deal easily in practice with the multiplicity that ensues. Multiplicity does not worry Mol for she believes it to be a feature of our lives that we cope with as an everyday matter. She is concerned instead with how we manage multiplicity without noticing. How, she asks, are the different versions of the one disease, made by practice in operating theatre and outpatients' clinic, able to hang together? What happens when the different versions are brought into one place? Or, to put it another way, how do we draw a picture of the multiple realities that exist, caused by different practices, but separated by only small spaces, times, or priorities? Her answer is that we find ways to spatially distribute, include within wholes, and place in hierarchies (Mol 2002). For Mol, multiple ways of performing a thing lead to multiple versions of that thing available to us. Following Mol, we would understand the multiplicity of my theories to be a natural consequence of embodied theory making.

## Justifying Multiplicity Two: Interpellation into Modes of Ordering

In the article, 'On the Subject of the Object', John Law provides another way to understand the multiplicity of data analysis (Law 2000). Again this is a consequence of practice, but one that comes by being pulled into already established theories. He talks of interpellation into modes of ordering. This is to use Louis Althusser's picture of state authority and ideology. Interpellation for Althusser means to find oneself part of the relations of power as soon as action is taken to pull you in. A policeman calls 'hey you', and you, in turning, become subject to him; subject to the material and ideological structures of the state (Althusser 1977: 160–165). By using this notion, Law refers to the fact that certain ways of enacting reality might call to us, 'hey you', making us in the moment of our acknowledgement subjected to their power (Law 2000: 13–15; see also Butler 1995; Verran 2001: 101–104).

It is this way when I am piling my cards. These theories do not come from nowhere, but from the talk of teachers and the writings of various theorists. It feels as if knowing these theories and the resonances they have in schools makes me receptive to the calls of pictures to be fitted into those patterns. It feels that, in knowing the relations of parts to whole in these various theories, each picture becomes interpellated into its place as soon as the theory comes to my mind.

Law illustrates the multiplicity of potential interpellations by telling the story of writing, or trying to write, the history of a military plane. This account became impossible for him to complete, and he writes to understand why this might have been. Part of his explanation is that he, his embodied mind, was being pulled into the various and mutually exclusive accounts and desires circulating around the aircraft. Should he write a 'plain history', a view-from-nowhere story about the historical trajectory of the craft? Should he write a policy history, detailing why the plane had been decommissioned and recommending ways to avoid such future losses? This was what many of his informants seemed to be expecting, but this was not what he wanted to add to the world. Should he write in an ethical mode, telling a story of the iniquities of the bomber in relation to the military industrial complex? This was a story deeply embedded within him already from exposure to the leftist political movements of the 1970s and 80s. Or perhaps he should write in an academic mode, telling the story in the particular disembodied language of the professional sociologist, a group to which he belonged. Maybe he should write this as an aesthetic story, telling of the power and even beauty of the machine that had called him, years before, to study it? These were some of the paths he felt pulled down, some stories he felt compelled by persons and objects to tell. But they were incompatible. Eventually he told the story of the aircraft in several ways, including this one of interpellation into multiple accounts (Law 2000: 19–23; see also Law 2002a; Law 2002b). Instead of hiding the multiplicity and the personal, ethical conflict he faced, he made it the subject of his enquiry. There is a suggestion implicit here. If he experienced multiplicity in writing his data, perhaps so do others. Perhaps it is a consequence of the way the world is, not of our inadequacies as clear thinkers. This suggests that we should talk about how to deal with multiplicity in theory making.

## Justifying Multiplicity Three: A Consequence of Ironic Understanding

Kieran Egan suggests a different way to think about multiplicity: as ironic understanding. His work is useful because it suggest that we in the twenty-first century might be getting better at recognising and dealing with explicit multiplicity. Egan tells a history of ways of thinking. In it we have now reached a stage of literacy that finds us distrusting the completeness of language and yet still participating in it. Just think of a person doing a Google search, dealing with the many pages of text that are flattened together into equality, but some more accurate and some more useful to their task. That person copes with the partiality and multiplicity of the results with their critical and selective gaze – their ironic understanding.

To understand what Egan means by ironic understanding and what it has to do with multiplicity, we need to draw in his larger theory of thinking. In his 1997 book, *The Educated Mind*, Egan expands and clarifies his argument that children's learning ideally recapitulates the changes in understanding that are visible in the historical record of Western civilisation. His argument rests on the idea that kinds of understanding are linked to our facility to use language.

We are more capable of different thinking when we have the tool of written language than when we have only oral language, for example. Egan explains that

> [k]inds of understanding are just the ways the mind works when using particular tools. All the kinds of understanding are potential or embryonic in all minds, along with an indeterminate range of other kinds of understanding that are so little evoked in our cultural environments that we hardly can recognize them (Egan 1997: 176).

Importantly, we retain the ability to perform each stage of thinking even when a new stage is achieved. Some losses of attention, skill, and interest are always to be experienced, but these can, and should be, minimised. Education should, he argues, be conceived as the appropriate encouragement of the 'kind of understanding' suitable to the stage a class has reached. I would like to remind readers at this point that Egan's are *intentionally* made, as are the broadest claims and the biggest pictures of incredibly complex histories and learning experiences. His basic scheme, massively simplified, is as follows:

Pre-language – Somatic Understanding
Oral language – Mythic Understanding
Early written language – Romantic Understanding
Sophisticated written language – Philosophic Understanding
Distrust of language itself – Ironic Understanding

Egan adds another column to this table. He suggests that we can understand Western intellectual history as the process of Western culture moving through these stages (the idea that children recapitulate the history of Western thought as they learn has been developed and defended throughout Egan's work. See Egan 1990; 1992; 2000). In *The Educated Mind*, he uses figures in Greek intellectual history that stand as having made the leaps required to move from one to the next. Mythic understanding, he suggests, is ubiquitous in cultures without written language. It remains so, in the stories we are all familiar with from our childhoods and in many of our other stories (on television, for example).

Romantic understanding can be seen in Herodotus's *History*. This he explains as being history interested in truth *and* extremes of human culture, biology, and feats. During romantic understanding, children might be drawn to the Guinness Book of World Records, to heroes, and to human agents as causes of historical changes. Philosophic understandings are those buildings of systems, those searching for laws, and cravings for certainty that Thucydides stands for, and which dominated intellectual endeavour in the nineteenth century. And ironic understanding is figured according to Egan by the ever-questioning Socrates, who was always denying the certainty of his knowledge even while he clearly did know much.

Over the twentieth century and into the twenty-first, as texts have proliferated and their authority and certainty questioned, ironic understanding has spread. To some extent this was brought into common consciousness by the post-modern concern with the limits of language. With ironic understanding we become more used to dealing with multiple accounts, their truths, and their differences. Perhaps (and this is me, not Egan), we have come to be more accepting of multiple accounts as we have become more used to the 'democratic' flattening of texts and authority with our new technologies: iPads, YouTube, Google searches, Internet news (for a related argument about flattening, see Law 2008). For Egan, ironic understanding does not need to flounder in the sense of uncertainty that this recognition brings. Instead, like Verran, he finds the process of being weaned away from certainty to be a good thing. For him, ironic understanding should be greeted with the 'flexible, buoyant recognition of a multi-vocal world, both within and without' (Egan 1997: 155).

## MULTIPLE THEORIES

With this optimistic vision of multiplicity, let us return to the picture of me piling cards – making theories and thus ontologically different 'imaginations'. Well, what did these piles look like? What theoretical arguments was I slotting into? And what would the implications of each be?

## Pile One: Imagination and Generalisations

In one attempt at piling, tempting for its binary nature and apparent simplicity, I found I could build two main groupings – a tree with two branches. In one pile would go all the pictures that seemed to tell only about personal experiences, taking quite literally the question 'a time you used your imagination'. These could then be sub-grouped into categories that I could gloss as absorption of self into other media (TV, movies, books, computer games); recall of past personal event (for example, imagining the fish to be caught while the line was in the water); projection of self into possible future (winning a swimming trophy); and projection of self into myth (riding a dragon).

Into the second core pile would go those that seemed to reflect on what imagination is, showing children themselves abstracting from what they had done, seen, or heard about imagination, and generalising about imagination as a concept. This pile could be broken into two further subgroups. In one went pictures that suggested imagination and creativity were the same. For example, several show groups of children doing art, carrying the implication that 'we always imagine in art'. The other group pictured various ways of crossing conceptual boundaries, suggesting a generalisation that saw imagination as a faculty that looks upon the categories of the world and enables their humorous mixing ('a monkey living in a house and a human being in a tree'). This distinction between the personal and the generalising did seem to work – most pictures were easy to categorise somewhere and all were possible to categorise. However, the system as a whole I found discomforting and I soon realised why: I had been interpellated into a building a Piagetian theory.

Jean Piaget worked in the mid-twentieth century building theories about children's cognitive development that had much to do with the late nineteenth century, and everything to do with the Euro-American conviction that science was the ultimate human achievement (Kitchener 1986. For a powerful critique of Piaget, see Walkerdine 1988). This rested on three assumptions we ought to

(Harry Potter)
A gryffindor table
in the great hall
with desserts/Hogwarts

**FIG. 3** Imagination as the Particular Experience of Absorption of Self into Harry Potter
Image reads: '(Harry Potter) A Gryffindor table in the great hall with desserts/
Hogwarts'

**FIG. 4** Imagination as the General Experience of Reading any Book
Images to show imagination as particular and generalised experience

be wary of. The first, coming out of the metaphysics that separates the world from knowers, assumes that scientific representations of the singular truth about the world are possible. The second follows on from this, taking as obvious that these truths are the highest goal for individual knowers and society alike. The third sees knowing as primarily involving disembodied minds (see Mol 2002: 153–157). In Piaget's version, children's cognitive function (their ability to think) would gradually develop towards this single goal of scientific knowing. Piaget described his aim as 'to study the origins of the various kinds of knowledge, starting with their most elementary forms, and to follow their development to later levels *up to and including scientific thought*' (quoted in Kitchener 1986: 4, emphasis added).

What would be wrong with accepting that this holds true in the primary schools I participated in? Please note that I am making an unfamiliar move here. I am not suggesting that Piaget's work is necessarily wrong. It is likely that children who are better at generalising will be better at science, and this capacity tends to increase with age. Perhaps also, science is the most sophisticated form of human thinking. Nor am I suggesting that Piaget's theories are unimportant in what goes on at primary schools, for it is certainly part of the tacit knowledge that teachers bring to their classroom practice. Indeed, on occasion teachers do re-enact the Piagetian division of children's intelligence based on their ability to theorise. In one lesson, for example, children made Plasticine symbols of the story they had just heard. The teacher used this as a diagnostic tool, pointing out to me the most 'advanced' children – those who had generalised the best (Catholic School, author field notes, 6 September 2007).

My discomfort sprang rather from the realisation that I would be *re*-enacting Piaget's theory wholesale, looking backwards to find a theory to place on top of the practices I had observed. I would be imposing a previous picture of reality suitable perhaps for its time and place, upon the practices of quite a different time and place. This would, firstly, shut down enquiry. There would be nothing much more to say, apart from that some children are better at generalising than others. But given this theory was developed by a scientific thinker, and being used by someone trained in analytic if not scientific thought, all this would say is 'these children are like me'. I am good at generalising, I am intelligent, therefore anyone like me is intelligent and anyone unlike me – i.e. bad at generalising – is not.

More, this arrogance would devalue the pictures (and hence development) of many of the children, including all those at Steiner school. A major part of Steiner educational theory argues that children are not able to think abstractly until the age of fourteen (Harwood 1958; see also chapter four of this work), and certainly the Steiner children I got to know were never encouraged to abstract while I was there. To adopt this form of theorising would be to suggest that Steiner children were at a lower cognitive level than others, despite their many other abilities and their general physical and mental equality with the rest of their age cohort. This would be single-minded and unfair – amounting to an IQ test of my own devising that marked some children high and others low.

It would also be bad for my research. I would be fixing myself, and my school participants, in (and as doing) a single reality – developing scientific thinking. I would then be unable to see what is clever, interesting, and important about their pictures. This would not adequately show the complexities of practice; complexities that were evident as I saw I could pile my cards differently.

## Pile Two: Imagination and Typologies

> Un-piling and re-piling I found a new pattern. This saw the cards divided into eight piles, each of which had children doing different types/methods of imagining. So children could be seen as doing imagination as: memory, self-fantasy, mythic fantasy, absorption, memory/reflection on creativity, memory/reflection on absorption, transcending the limits of the situation, and humour/play with categories.
>
> This piling also worked in that cards seemed to fit somewhere (sometimes in two groups) and none were left out. But again I realised I was drawing on a theoretical position, and again I was discomforted by what I would be doing if I let this patterning rest.

Building typologies is commonplace in data analysis and theorising, and indeed is a useful technique for thinking with. In the case of imagination, typologies

have been necessary for trying to unravel the obvious complexity and multiplicity that greet us when we start to think about how the word is used in our lives. Imagination can be used to talk about creativity, fantasy, lies, goal making, re-creating vivid memories, planning, and many other things. But, as Raymond Williams says, 'there is a problem in using not just the same word but the same concept' for all the various manifestations of imagination (Williams 1991: 267). Moreover, this variety seems to call out for ordering. In a classic phenomenological version, Sartre (1948) gives an outline of the types of imagination as he experienced them. And more recently, McGinn stated that 'it is difficult to approach systematically, to impose order on the various manifestations of imagination. That is what I have attempted in this book' (McGinn 2004: iv).

In themselves, these works need not be worrying if they remained reflections on their authors' own imagination – a topic everyone is uniquely able to speak about. There is a problem, however, in assuming that one's own mental processes are like those of all others. This might be the case, but it is far from certain, and even more uncertain when one is talking about people living in different times and places from oneself. And, of course, in research interested in practice, minds are not even particularly relevant: action is.

Moreover, typographies seldom rest at division into difference: they are easily turned into hierarchies. Thus, Sartre distinguishes between good and bad imaginations; Williams argues that only one type of imagination really deserves the name; and McGinn devises a spectrum of imagination as shades of increasing sophistication (Sartre 1948; Williams 1991; McGinn 2004). This temptation is not incidental to the typographical approach; rather it occurs as a result of the search to reduce complexity – what is the best imagination, what is imagination 'really'? This is intrinsic to universalism: there might be multiple types or multiple meanings of imagination, but generally, one is more truly imaginative or more truly good.

Typologies of imagination are also built into school days. Just as art is done in a different room from mathematics, creative expression is kept out of maths, and mental representations of the abstract are kept out of art. Making up an imaginative game is to be done only in the playground and at break times, not in the more serious class time. Drama, the embodiment of another character, is a Friday afternoon treat.

It is exactly this tendency to divide one imagination from another that I wish to avoid. Not only does it collapse the multiplicities and complexities of practice into confusing examples of some single typographical system (even if my own), but this would also tempt me into blindness when it comes to things that don't seem to fit, or to force them into fitting. It would also claim that other minds are like my own and divide things in the same way. My ways of dividing imagination are, however, a product of my specific times and places – books read, schools attended, friends talked to.

## Pile Three: Imagination and Meaning

This would not do. So again I tried, looking, thinking and piling, making patterns emerge. In the theory I played out this time, children are seen as having each drawn a meaning of imagination. Each has told me what (perhaps among other things) imagination means to them. These too could be grouped, with more categories needed and more pictures that seemed to fit in more than one category. I found pictures that could be read as saying imagination is something that helps us play; enables us to create stories and pictures; gives us historical empathy; lets us transcend the frustrations of our situation; and many others. I felt much more comfortable now – I was giving agency and voice to my participants – but still I was perplexed and doubtful.

The theoretical format I am adopting here is one which an anthropologist might use. In *grounded theory* for example, a qualitative researcher would attempt to gain an understanding of the perspectives that their research subjects had – to find what meanings the world had for the people being studied. As Kathy Charmaz, one of the most prolific anthropologists to write about grounded theory as well as use it, puts it, grounded theory 'celebrates first hand knowledge of empirical worlds [...][it] aims toward interpretive understanding of subjects' meanings' (Charmaz 2000: 510). This is a good approach in terms of the ethics of fieldwork – respecting the 'world views' of participants.

**FIG. 7** Imagination as Meaning Play with Categories
Image reads (with spelling corrected): 'I am drawing a picture of a monkey living in a house and a human living in a tree instead of a monkey in a tree and a human in a house'

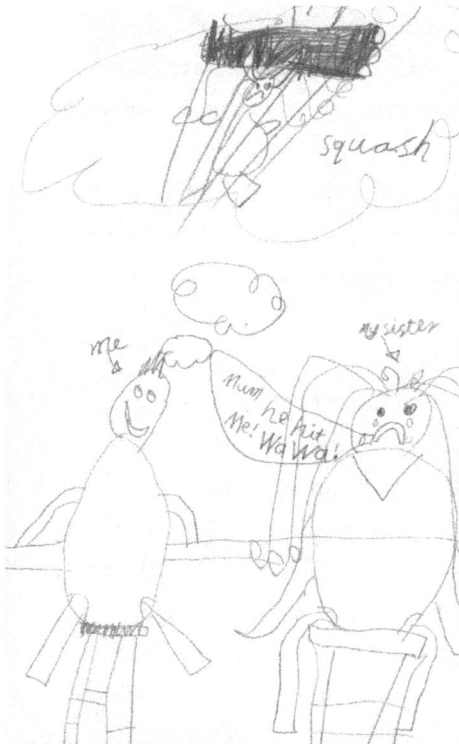

**FIG. 8** Imagination as Meaning Transcending the Frustrations of a Situation by Dropping a Chair on an Annoying Sister
Images to show imagination as having meaning

But it has to be used carefully, for it gets things the wrong way around. If we engage in looking at practice, we see that meaning doesn't cause practice: it is caused, enacted, and changed *in* practice (for more on this idea see chapter two). Imagination, this view tells us, is not something out there, a real and fixed part of people's minds and lives, waiting to be represented. Nor is imagination simply a concept constructed by children – or more conventionally, constructed and taught by the adults around them.

Instead it is something that is enacted in practice – sometimes, perhaps usually, resonating with the definitions that people will speak or write, not because they are 'correct' or because they are speaking for their language or culture, but because material arrangements, habits of word and gesture, and the organisation of school time allow certain practices to occur and be prioritised.

Looking at these pictures as simply telling us about meaning would give us two options. Either we would have to see them as better or worse accounts of the universal meaning of imagination, or as better or worse representations of the many equally valid socially constructed meanings of imagination. It would ignore the practices the children had depicted, casting them as simple scene-setting or as explanatory devices. It would see the materials and differing teacher instructions as limits to the cross-school comparability of the pictures, not as practices of interest in themselves. Our task would be to see through the pictures into what the children were really trying to say: which meaning of imagination were they trying to articulate? Where did the 'real' meaning of imagination, purified of technology and practice, rest for each child?

This approach would furthermore fall into the metaphysics that Verran has tried to make explicit and thereby refuse. We are very used to taking for granted the tripartite division between the world, representations of the world (knowledge), and knowers in whose minds knowledge is made and the world judged. If we took the search for meaning as our methodological basis, we would be making this tripartite division. We would have to see me, a researcher, removed from and judging the participants in my study (children and teachers). I would be separate from my world of knowers, seeing them from a distance. Those knowers, the children and teachers, would be assumed to see 'imagination' from a distance as either a single object seen from different perspectives, or as a cultural construct. They would be separate from their object of knowledge – 'imagination'. I would be separate from the children and teachers, who would be separate from imagination. I would be looking at them looking at imagination. This would give me the role of maker of judgement, ignoring my own participation in the enactments of imagination at these schools *and* the fact that I am enacting a version of truth suitable to a particular university discipline at a particular time and place. It would fail to meet Addelson's standards for ethical double participation (1994: 160–182).

## Pile Four: Imagination and the Politics of Becoming

> So with these worries sensed but unarticulated, I decomposed the piles again, sitting with the whole lot and simply looking. Suddenly striking this time were the pictures that didn't seem to quite fit my expectations – those that surprised and confused. There was one that showed two children and a house, captioned 'when I was doing a dance with my friends'. A practice of embodied imagination, perhaps. Another was of a computer screen with a maze-like game on it; imagining with a computer, a child made cyborg. A third showed a road, trees, and snake but not as a scaled or representative view but which (to me) captured a feeling. Imagination as bodily affect felt when going bush with dad?

These three pictures, and others too, showed practices and linked them to imagination. They were an expression of imaginations that had emerged in doings, and which are not contained in what observers and theorists say about imagination.

What would I be claiming about imagination if I took this piling seriously? All these pictures are about children's bodily interactions with parts of the human and non-human world. They seem to be about the new and surprising products of these interactions, be they dances, understanding of the structure of a computer game, or the emotions conjured by being in the wilds of Australia. So these pictures show imagination as the unpredictable outcomes of human and non-human interactions. These may only last a moment, but can stay with us in memory.

**FIG. 9** Imagination as a Feeling
The image reads: 'This picture is about when me and my dad go into the bush I imagine'.

**FIG. 10** Embodied Imagination
The image reads: When I was doing a dance with my friends
Images to show imagination as the emerging new

When examined in this light, the other pictures made sense also. They too were about interactions with other humans and/or non-humans, and they were about the outcomes of these interactions. The difference was that these others pictured interactions and outcomes that were more familiar. They told us about outcomes we have already cemented in our culture as being about imagination. Art, we are used to thinking, is about imagination; so too is the fantasy of winning a swimming competition, and pretending it is oneself who is riding the dragon from the story. In other words, these pictures hid the fact that they were about the outcomes of unpredictable interactions, because we have seen and articulated those interactions before. Having done so does not mean that we would have been able to predict it, just that when it occurs we know what to call it.

To theorise imagination in this way is, just as before, to invite consequences. Now they are for how we should do academic work. They are consequences that implicate a type of politics. I will follow Andrew Pickering and call this a politics of experimentation. By this he means to 'imaginatively and critically explore the open-ended spaces of the world's possibility' (Pickering 2008: 13). Doing this kind of politics well requires engaging in a new and difficult way of seeing and talking that Verran, Mol and Law, and Star can help us with.

This politics, I suggest, has three main elements. The first, articulated best by Verran, is that we should engage with what is new and momentary. These can be recognised more easily at some points than others: for Verran what is of interest are the moments when people with different ontological commitments meet and try to work together. She calls these 'postcolonial moments' (Verran 2002: 730; Verran 2004). What comes out of such moments are the type of open-ended possibilities that Pickering speaks of. So too with imagination – we should work to notice the outcomes when people work with humans, places, and technologies that are unfamiliar. The unfamiliar demands an imaginative response if people are to find ways to live and work with them. The outcomes of these interactions, however, might be novel, fleeting, and difficult to grasp.

The second element in Pickering's politics is to engage in what Mol and Law call 'ontological politics'. To some extent, I will treat this as a caveat for the first part of our critical arsenal. This term was first coined by Mol in 1999 and later adopted by Law (2004). By ontological politics they mean that we must be aware that 'reality does not precede the mundane practices in which we interact with it, but is rather shaped within these practices' (Mol 1999: 75). Ontological politics helps us recognise that the agents involved in imagining are already being shaped by the reality they live with, and the practices this reality is made by. Their choices about what to do with their imaginations are already limited by their practical lives. Teachers, for example, have to choose to follow the curriculum to some extent. Children have to choose to accept this as their learning, or face punishments. PhD candidates have to choose to write in ways that are accepted by supervisors and examiners, and authors in ways that their publishers and publics will like. This means that the possibilities of the world are not so open-ended as we might hope, but the ways in which they are closed are particular to differently practising agents.

Finally, and with Susan Leigh Star, to do Pickering's politics we must be ready to attempt to articulate that which is difficult or impossible to articulate, including when we follow the conventions of academic writing. Star explores an aspect of this problem in a beautiful piece about the experience of pain. Her suggestion is that underlying much of science and social science is the aim to generalise experience. But there are experiences that one can only know in the particular. One aim of social science therefore should be to tell of experience in such a way that it is generalisable, that captures a collective experience, by choosing sometimes to tell of the particular and momentary: 'Responding to experience means letting generalization and specificity be in dialectic in our writings and biographies' (Star 1998: 144). This is what Pickering asks in calling for *imaginative* exploration of the world's open-ended possibilities. Sometimes the one, used imaginatively, can tell us about the many.

## CONCLUSION

I began this chapter by arguing for the bodily nature of data analysis and theory building. This, I have said, naturally leads to multiplicity. Multiplicity, I have gone on to say, is not in itself a problem. Rather it is something we should think carefully about how to deal with. In this case, I have argued, multiple theories of imagination are not wrong. Each represents some of what goes on in class-rooms and makes sense in broader theoretical traditions. But each has ethical and political consequences that we need to be conscious of if we are to make good decisions about which to endorse, particularly if we think our writing might have consequences for what happens in schools.

In this case I have argued that a politics of experimentation, enacted by theorising imagination as the unpredictable outcome of human and non-human interactions, is the most ethical. This is partly because (I believe) it is the most accurate: it gels with the metaphysics I follow throughout this book that tells reality as emergent in practice. But it is also the most ethical because it returns a type of integrity to the work of social science. By focusing on what is new, on what is possible and not possible for particular agents, and by striving to find new ways to articulate the experience of us all, the politics of experimentation is one that engages with people and things struggling to speak, act, and imagine anew.

PART TWO

# IMAGINATION IN CLASSROOM PRACTICE

**4**

# PICTURES IN THE MIND

*A Steiner Classroom and Representational Imagination*

Every morning begins the same way. Children who have been playing in the classroom go out the door and line up. The senior teacher, Shirley, stands at the entrance. When she decides the children are neat and quiet, she lets them move forward, one by one, to shake her hand. One by one they enter the room, walk across, and shake assistant teacher Paul's hand and then my own. With each shake they greet and are greeted by name. Once they have done this, they form a circle: 'Quietly', Shirley reminds. They begin to sing 'Morning has Broken'. After a series of songs (some sung in rounds) they might recite a poem, chant together a times-table, or learn a simple circle dance. When this is complete they sit on the mat, still in a circle, to identify which students are not at school today and to hear the day's timetable and notices. Then, after a break to go to the bathroom, they sit again on the mat, wherever they choose now, for the morning story. In the practice of telling the morning story, we will watch imagination being made: a set of bodily routines that call up pictures in the minds of the students.

WE MET THIS TEACHER, SHIRLEY, IN THE INTRODUCTION. THERE SHE TOLD us that young people's imagination is our hope for solving social, economic, and environmental problems. Now we will see how she works in practice to teach her students how to do an imagination that might generate these wholly new solutions. And readers might be surprised, as I was, to find that key to the practice of imagination here is representation.

Teaching imagination in this classroom means teaching children to do the Platonic job of projecting images on the walls of their minds to bridge the gap between the world 'out there' and our knowledge 'in here'. Only when children have realised themselves as capable of representing the concrete world in this way might they become able to further realise themselves as capable of abstract thought. Because of the centrality of imagination as representation in this classroom, I too perform some representation.

This performance is play, and dangerous play, as I will show at the end of the chapter. There is much that slips out from underneath these representations when we are honest about our own situated and emotional experience of the events we seek to represent. Thus readers are reminded that representational imagination is a performance – as are the other modes of imagination I discuss.

I will include in this chapter something usually edited out: my at times strong emotional reactions to the classroom practices I was involved with. While this is often implicit, it is included to remind readers that I betray the picture of social science researcher as unbiased objective observer and recorder of facts. I neither pretend to be a removed, judging observer nor aim to represent what happened. I do not ask 'is the imagination I met in this Steiner classroom a true representation of real imagination?'

Exploring what this representational imagination is and how it is done will be my first task. I do this by making the morning story stand for – represent – what imagination is in this classroom more generally. For teachers in this class, the representational imagination is a central element of what makes this education distinct from others. Seeing how teachers describe their own work will be the second task of this chapter. In the third section, I will draw a comparison between this way of representing teaching and one articulated as 'mainstream'. This is based on specific and differing visions of the 'natural child'. Each of these three sections will do a version of representation: in the first, certain events are made to stand for the whole; in the second, imagination is used by teachers to symbolise their educational traditions; and in the third, modes of imagining are used to stand for good and bad education in the local media. Focusing on representation in this way is part of my work to give a symmetrical account of my classrooms. I talk about representation because this is the imagination I see practised in this classroom. But I only go so far with this vision: in the concluding section, I discuss the limits of representation for making an ethical assessment of this classroom.

## IMAGINATION AS REPRESENTATION: PICTURES IN THE MIND

> Shirley, the teacher, is seated on a chair with the children gathered around her on the mat. She begins by recounting what happened in the story she told yesterday: Odin invited the gods to a feast but Baldur planned to disrupt it. Then she begins proper, with neither book nor props, to tell the story from her memory. This is strict: teachers do not read the story from a book because it must come 'alive' from the teachers' own mind when they memorise the story each night. They must 'clothe the story in their own mental pictures' (Steiner School, author interview with assistant teacher, 15 June 2007). As the teacher, either Paul or Shirley, tells the story, the children sit still and listen.

What we see during the morning story is a daily process designed to build in children particular mental pictures as well as the more general capacity to build such pictures. During the morning story, children are to imagine the narrated events as pictures in their minds. As Shirley tells it, imagination 'is very pictorial. [...] Even for aural people, there's always a picture element to it' (Steiner School, author interview with teacher, 15 June 2007). Visual representation in the mind is told here as the necessary element of imagination.

Imagination has long been associated with images in the mind of absent things. As Kant put it in the *Critique of Pure Reason*, '[i]magination is the faculty of representing in intuition an object that is not itself present' (Kant 1929:165). In its first syllable of imagination, 'image' is conjured. This idea is referred to in phrases like 'the mind's eye', and developed by associations between imagination and visualising, or picturing. This is to suggest that imagination is representation. This way of talking about imagination has led to work done in psychology and neuroscience designed to examine the physiological nature and limits of imagery (Kosslyn 1994; Frawley 1997). This leads also into the close associations made between imagination and fantasy, delusion, or hallucination that relate imagination to things pathological. These associations wonder about whether the picture in someone's imagination is a copy of something real or of something unreal mistaken for the real (see Woolley 1997; Hersch 2003).

As the morning story is told at Steiner school, there is no querying of its truth or falsity. Instead, for this grade, the Norse myths are told as if they are true, their artfulness never highlighted. In one story, when Odin whispers something to another character, Shirley reports that 'no one has ever known what that was' (Steiner School, author field notes, 6 June 2007). These are said to have happened 'a long time ago' (Steiner School, author field notes, 17 June 2007) and when a child asks where Denmark is, Shirley tells him that it is where the stories happened (Steiner School, author field notes, 7 June 2007). They are told as if they represent the past, not as if they represent some people's allegories, fears, or codes of behaviour. They are told as history, not as myth. This blurring of historical and mythical is considered unproblematic as long as the teacher has control of it. However, if children independently begin to believe that the unreal is real, teachers become concerned. They explain that worrying imagination is that which loosens its bond with the real to become fantasy or escapism. To have no basis in reality would be 'bizarre', 'not healthy or something' (Steiner School, author interview with assistant teacher, 15 June 2007). It would be to lose the 'moral element', to 'live some other weird parallel existence' (Steiner School, author interview with teacher, 15 June 2007).

The aim is not to encourage children to think critically about the stories; it is rather for them to feel an emotional response. In the Steiner tradition as Shirley reports it, emotionally charged mental pictures buttress the possibility for later learning. She explains the fundamentals of the education at this age as 'not about the intellect. It's about warm feelings and the imagination' (Steiner School, author field notes, 6 June 2007). It is commonplace in scholarship to associate the mental imagery with emotional affect. When we picture something we might also feel some reaction welling up. These links have been explored variously by Sartre (1948) and throughout the (psycho)analysis of dreams.

Imagination as copies of the world is assumed to open up into the world of unconscious or emotional personal meaning.

Children in this classroom are told as living in their imaginations. There is no separation made between the child at play and the child thinking: they are in imagination at all times. Thus, imagination is practised as the basis for learning in this classroom. As Shirley explains: 'Steiner said everything a child learns should be from the world and from [mental] pictures' (Steiner School, author field notes, 6 June 2007). These mental pictures, and the physical and verbal playing they might lead to, 'are the foundation of abstract thought' that will grow and take over from a predominately imaginative way of being in the world (Steiner School, author interview with teacher, 15 June 2007).

## Imagination at the Heart of Learning

Imagination, then, is taken to be the foundation for learning in this classroom. By what practices is this achieved? Teachers, I will argue here, have three sets of techniques to keep imagination at the heart of learning. These are to help children make their mental images concrete; to let children's knowledge flow from images, either concrete or mental; and let children learn from their concrete mental pictures instead of conceptualising.

The first techniques are those aimed at helping children to externalise their mental images. Drawing is a method for doing this, though it is not the only one. These children, to my eye, are very skilful representational artists, and this is partly due to the drawing lessons they receive, sometimes as part of their 'main lesson'. This is the core learning period of the day, undertaken in the morning while the children are believed to be freshest.

But drawing is just one way of making mental objects concrete. We see other methods during a lesson conducted when they are beginning project work. This lesson also shows the teachers' insistence that learning begin by externalising mental pictures. Each child chooses an animal for their project. Paul instructs them that it is very helpful to begin by imagining how their animal moves. They are asked to imagine a horse, and are talked through some words that describe a moving horse: gallop, canter, walk, trot, buck, run, rear (writing these on the board, Paul does not include suggested words from dressage or showjump-ing: these are not the movements of animals in nature). Next, some children are chosen to bodily imitate how a horse moves. They trot and canter in front of their classmates. These are ways of externalising the image of a horse using language and bodies. Next Paul moves onto the work that would be included in the physical project. He says, 'I'm going to get you to close your eyes and I'm going to give you two minutes to imagine how your animal moves'. Then straight away and without talking they are expected to start their drawings. After the two minutes is up a hand goes up. 'Can I use a book?' 'No,' Paul says, 'just from what you imagined,' and, touching his forehead, 'you have a picture in here' (Steiner School, author field notes, 7 June 2007).

Here we see several ways of making the mental pictures concrete, ranging from finding words to describe, performing mimes, and drawing. These have all begun with the instruction to imagine an animal, and, when it comes to draw-ing their own, they are told to focus, eyes closed, on this mental picture. And this, as I've indicated, is to be used as a starting point for their project learning. Gathering an understanding of the animal's movement by their mental picturing is to be a necessary condition for learning more factual information.

The primacy of picturing for later learning is highlighted when, after having been on a class trip to the zoo, several children decide to change the animal they are working on. Shirley tells them that they must start by drawing these new animals, even though the rest of the class are now reading for and writing in their projects. One boy decides that his project is now going to be about butterflies. Shirley asks, instructing, 'can you close your eyes and see how it moves?' She tells him that when she mentally sees a butterfly it is taking off from a flower. The boy replies that he mentally sees his butterfly flying. 'That's fine', Shirley says, emphasising that his picture should be different from hers because they are personal. Only then is he allowed to start making this mental picture concrete by drawing his imagined butterfly. He will be days behind his classmates in the project (Steiner School, author field notes, 17 June 2007).

What we see here is that learning in this classroom is to be made meaningful by the affective and personal moment of mentally picturing. We find this again and again in this class: long division is learnt by starting with a story about

Odin's feast; past, present, and future tense are introduced as three weaving goddesses from the Norse myths; years earlier they learnt the alphabet with the story of a gnome meeting letter-shaped obstacles (mountains like M's, valleys like V's). Only after these images have been formed in children's minds is the more formal learning to begin.

But crucially, and this is our third point, generalisations, objectifications, or conceptualisations are never the goal of formal Steiner learning. Understandings should be about the concrete or particular, not about the abstract or general. On my first day, Shirley reprimands me after a girl tells me her name is the same forwards and backwards, and I respond by saying that these are called palindromes (Steiner School, author field notes, 4 June 2007). This is considered bad because it conceptualises and generalises the particular experience of having such a name. This avoidance of concepts produces some strange results, since they are very hard to avoid altogether. Instead of dry categories from the outside world, children are taught to classify through their visual imaginations. For example, instead of learning about the zoological division of the animal kingdom, children learn to place animals in the categories of 'head', 'trunk' (or torso), and 'limb' animals. Which category animals will be placed in is to be obvious from the children's picturing of them, and seeing which anatomical part they seem to favour as they move. Picturing each particular animal will tell children where they should fit in the general scheme.

So in this Steiner classroom, imagination is practised as emotionally charged and personally meaningful copies of the real world. This is to form the basis of all later learning. Particular objects are not meant to stand for the abstract whole as at other schools, the learning is 'really' about the whole. Instead, pictures of concrete parts will eventually add up to emotionally meaningful pictures of concrete wholes.

Why is learning at this school practised in this way? If we listen to teachers we will learn that they believe their practices are a part of a particular philosophical tradition that includes a theory of child development and learning. As a result, their classroom represents the beliefs of Rudolf Steiner in its material arrangements. To express this vision, teachers use particular representations of imagination and of the natural child.

## STEINER SAYS: REPRESENTING TEACHING WORK

Teachers at this school tell me often about their teaching practice and beliefs with the phrase 'Steiner said'. Here are some: 'Steiner said that you must love the child for any teaching to happen'; 'Steiner said spirals are hygienic'; 'Steiner said everything the child learns must be from the world and from pictures' (Steiner School, author field notes, 5, 6, 7 June 2007). These are also used to explain the education to me during interviews. Paul tells me that 'this curriculum to me is based, Steiner says, on where the child is at that age, so there's this fit, not just with the head at that time, but what's going on with them emotionally and otherwise' (Steiner School, author interview with assistant teacher, 15 June 2007). Steiner's words are presented as making sense in relation to modern science and common sense. What he is said to have said is interwoven with the machinery of modern childhoods. Shirley tells me, for example, that

> Steiner indicated clearly, and other studies are now starting to talk about, that free imagination, that free play, that pure imaginative play is not playing Simba, you know, is not playing the *Lion King*, it's playing from one's own volition, that is the foundation for abstract thought (Steiner School, author interview with teacher, 15 June 2007).

In these quotes, teachers tell us that their teaching and curriculum, the routines of the school day, their focus on play and away from media, all represent the wisdom of Rudolf Steiner. They aim to re-create in their school the conditions that Steiner advocated for 'natural' child development (emotional and intellectual). The classroom this work takes part in is designed as a re-creation, a copy, of the classrooms that Steiner advocated as ideal. This ideal is one of the late nineteenth or early twentieth century. In its material and temporal arrangements, this classroom is intended to represent Steiner's vision.

> The children sit at their desks – which are wooden and made especially for use in Steiner schools – arranged in four rows. It is time for the main lesson held in the morning when children's learning is said to be the best. They are

asked to get out their equipment for writing: their wooden pencil boxes all bought from the same speciality shop and the fabric crayon holders they have made in craft lessons. These have a woven exterior and a cotton interior with separate pockets for each colour. No black crayon is included: Steiner said that children of this age are not ready for black. At the front, Paul opens out the hinged blackboard so that the two panels that have been visible reveal the four beneath. On one panel, he has drawn a penguin.

This school is materially equipped as a school might have been in late nineteenth century Europe, indeed as the primary school that Rudolf Steiner himself attended might have been. Blackboards, and crayons, and wooden desks; a brass bell; wooden play equipment, and knitted socks. At no point during the school day will children interact with articles made from synthetic materials. Instead, they are to occupy a world made from things that humans have been interacting with throughout the centuries of cultural evolution up to the end of the nineteenth century.

These material relations do more than produce a child as part of an older world. They also work to build the child's physical senses of the natural world, unmediated by the materials of the largely human-made contemporary world. And they form one side of a dualism of the familiar nature/culture dualism, as we shall see in more detail in the next section. This is then connected to the experience/concepts dichotomy. Knowing nature via experience is to form the basis for 'real' imagination as opposed to the meaningless escapism of our culture's conceptual imagination. We experience nature directly, therefore it is real. We do not experience concepts, therefore they are not. It is for this reason that computers and television are strongly discouraged, and these, along with books, are never used by the teacher as teaching aids (this is not a complete ban: children are encouraged to read at nine years though not explicitly taught, and use books from the school library for their projects.) The experience/concepts dualism is also the reason that I am asked not to speak in terms that objectify real experiences – not to tell children the word 'palindrome' after they boast of names that are the same backwards as forwards. This is what Shirley means when she says that free imagination rather than playing *The Lion King* is the foundation for abstract thought. It is also why imagination for Shirley never strays from the real, and when the stories told are really myths, their mythical nature is ignored.

What these material arrangements and avoidance of modern culture represent is a particular notion of the natural child. What is a child and what is their natural potential? What do they need and what must they avoid in order to develop naturally? These questions are central to the educational endeavour. The premises about child naturalness that schools run on are taken as obvious to those involved. Sometimes, however, answers clash.

This happened in a series of newspaper reports published in the year I undertook my research.

## TELLING THE NATURAL CHILD

These reports flared with the contestation over running Steiner classrooms in Victorian government schools. While Steiner schools have run in Australia since the 1950s, until the late 1990s they operated as institutions providing an alternative type of education (for a history of Steiner education in Australia, see Whitehead 2004). In the late 1990s, a Melbourne school, Footscray City Primary, proposed opening a Steiner stream. This proposal was subject to investigation and report by the local office of the State Department of Education. The authors of the report, Janette Cook and Pat Hincks, recommended that the proposal be rejected. Regardless, the school opened its Steiner stream in 2001. Now Steiner education was being offered as an alternative educational philosophy within government schools instead of an alternative to the government sanctioned education system (Rood 2006: 11).

The Victorian State government officially legitimised the education in a policy released in September 2006 allowing Steiner streams to be run in government schools, but during the subsequent years, the programmes caused division between parents and schools. One such conflict was taken by a parent to the national newspaper, *The Australian* (Rout 2007: 3). Accompanying this report was a photo of a Steiner classroom that I recognised as the grade three classroom of the school I worked in. The photo, however, was mislabelled and said to represent a classroom in a Sydney Steiner school. This mistake may not have mattered to many people – the photo was intended to represent Steiner schools as a general category, not any one particular Steiner class or school. The report did the same: what was said of one parent's experience of a particular Steiner classroom was to be read as pertaining to all Steiner schools. That the category 'Steiner School' calls up universalist thinking is not noticeable unless one knows about the concrete here-and-now of Steiner practice.

The report opens, significantly, with the story of a father's shock that his son was to repeat a grade because his soul had not yet fully incarnated. This is a discourse about what should be important in a stage model of child development. That which the Steiner philosophy was told as operating on – a stage model that takes souls into consideration – was in opposition to that of this boy's father. 'I just looked at my wife and we both thought, "We are out of here"' (Rout 2007: 3).

The article tells us more about the stage model underlying Steiner practice: age restrictions on the use of crayon colours, only reading and writing after age seven, discourses of 'emerging personalities' and developing children's senses of the physical world. It tells us what is deemed by its authors to be notable or odd things about the Steiner logic of child development.

Two aspects of these stages are explicitly compared to the expectations of government schools. One is the restriction of literacy: the '"antithesis" of the government program'. The other is the ban on computers and multimedia, 'in "direct contradiction" to departmental policy'. In both these examples, appeal is made to readers' sense of developmental stages, with the norm presented as that of the government. Steiner stages are 'the antithesis' of the norm, are in 'direct contradiction' to the norm, and this language helps to produce those norms. The article goes on, quoting at greater length the 2000 report that opposed Footscray's request for a Steiner stream. '"Steiner education is based on a philosophy of cocooning children from the world to develop their imagination," the report says. "This is in direct contrast to, for example, the studies of society and environment [ ... ] where the emphasis is on the study of family as a 'starting point to help them understand the world in which they live"' (Rout 2007: 3).

Right here this article articulates the two themes central to the dispute between the stage models of imagination operating in Steiner and government schools. At Steiner schools, readers are told, children are 'cocooned from the world'. Additionally, according to this report, children at Steiner schools 'develop their imaginations' whereas children at state schools engage in 'studies'. Here we find a division made between the softness of developing imaginations and the rationality of study. So, not only we do learn much about the competing stage models of these two educational practices, we learn too that the debate between Steiner and government approaches is represented in the public realm as sourced from competing stage models of what is 'natural' child development.

What is being contested, in part, are representations of the 'natural child'. Central to the dispute are considerations of what the child's imagination should be. This turns on two issues. What is the relationship between the child and the social and adult world? And should the child's learning begin from inside or outside a person? Steiner schools are told as envisaging a child kept separate from the adult social world and whose learning begins from their emotional centre. They should freely imagine, not rationally think. Government schools, by contrast, are told as envisaging a child for whom the social and adult world is natural, and whose learning begins from their interactions with this world. We see these two issues refracted through the contrasting models of the natural child.

I begin by exploring the developmental logic that governs the practices of imagination at this Steiner school.

## The Natural Steiner Child: Imagination and Stages of Development

Quite explicitly, Rudolf Steiner saw in his own life a model both of how humans naturally develop and of what transformation they should strive for. These are told as insights from much before the first Waldorf (Steiner) School was set up in 1919, and before he become associated with the spiritual movement Theosophy. Steiner dates his understanding of the task of education to his early twenties. In 1884, Steiner was employed as a tutor for the Specht family, the youngest of whom suffered from what we would probably now call hydrocephaly. From this experience, he reports bringing away a keen sense of what humans were like – a combination of body and spirit – and prescriptions of how education should therefore proceed.

[With the hydrocphalitic student] I had to find access to a soul that was in a sleeping condition and that gradually had to be brought to master the bodily functions. [...] The educational method I had to adopt gave me insight into the way man's soul and spirit are connected with his bodily nature. It became my actual training in physiology and psychology. I came to realise that education and teaching must become an art, based upon true knowledge of man (Steiner 1977: 96–97).

Thus, education for Steiner relied on a joining of body, soul, and mind.

Steiner's educational theory was also related to a stage model of how children developed towards the spirited body – the body with soul. In cycles of seven years, children would gradually come to have access through their 'imaginative cognition' to the spiritual world. 'Imaginative cognition is nothing more than those forces whose spiritual activity forms the human body and soul from puberty until the age of twenty' (Steiner 1997: 114). Moving through their natural cycles, children would be recapitulating the supposed history of the human race before the mistaken recent past of materialism. These children would complete the transition that Steiner was convinced must be occurring during his era, escaping the entrapment of the simply bodily and moving beyond into the spiritual realm.

The cycles referred to here are intrinsic to the Steiner educational, as well as wider philosophy. A. C. Harwood, who opened the first Steiner school in the United Kingdom and helped reintroduce Steiner schools to Germany after 1945, describes these cycles in his study of Steiner's educational philosophy, *The Recovery of Man in Childhood* (Harwood 1958). This book, recommended to me by Paul, the assistant teacher, outlines the processes of child development. In the first seven years, children are driven by their will, using the extension of the limbs to attain the satisfaction of their desires. From the age of seven until the age of fourteen, the child is said to be driven by their emotional and imaginative life, their heart. Once they reach fourteen, their minds will begin to develop the capacity for abstract thought. Their learning should likewise move from the wilful and emotional heart towards the mental. In our classroom, the children's reports are based on this model.

There is a collective purpose to this education, tied to the belief in a historical transformation towards a philosophically non-materialist world and the spiritual potential of every human imagination. These beliefs are never spoken of in this classroom, but do animate the logic of the education. Believing deeply in his ability to access the inner world of the spirits through meditation, the sighting of auras, and communication with the dead, Steiner came to believe he was a prophet of the new age. Like him, we could

> obtain imaginative cognition when we systematically do quite specific meditations that I describe in the above-named books [*How to Know Higher Worlds* and *Outline of Occult Science*], when we train thinking beyond the level of normal life and conventional science. Imaginative cognition first gives us the possibility of developing pictures in our soul life, pictures that are not spatial, not fantasy, but that *represent* spiritual reality (Steiner 1997: 111, emphasis in original).

An ability to form mental pictures would be necessary to gain spiritual enlightenment.

So we find here the logic of Steiner's natural child development, consisting in a picture of seven-year cycles, the ideal adult, and the idea of recapitulating human history without becoming stuck in the materialism Steiner abhorred. Imagination will develop over the life course in terms of what it *represents*, starting with the physical, moving into the emotional, then the abstract, and finally to the realm of the spiritual.

## Constructing Embodied Brains:
## Stages of Development in 'Mainstream' Schools

How does this differ from representations of the 'natural child' by the Victorian state government? There children are told as 'naturally social'. We find a clear articulation of this in the Victorian Essential Learning Standards, or VELS, the latest curriculum being used at Victorian schools. This not only represents the 'natural child' but provides the machinery for the production of that 'natural child' through their schooling. In VELS no intrinsic separation is made between the child and adult worlds. Instead, the child is to learn from exposure to the world outside their bodies.

As told in VELS, the logic of the developing child moves through a three-stage model that roughly corresponds to childhood (ages five to ten), puberty (eleven to fifteen), and early adulthood (sixteen and seventeen). Constructivism is entrenched in the language of VELS. Primary school aged children, years 'prep' (preparatory) to grade four, are 'laying the foundations', prior to 'building breadth and depth'. Learning is told as equivalent to brain development. The two, knowledge and brain development, are told as processes that mirror each other. Just as brains are built as networks of neurons, so knowledge is built as networks of ideas. Learning will not happen unless information has a network of neurons to attach to. As it is said in the 'Thinking Skills' section, broken down into stages of learning, 'Information enters the brain through existing networks of neurons. It is these existing networks, this prior knowledge, which is the basis for constructing new understanding'.* For this building, the VELS child will call on experience, not just of the natural world, but also social and fantasy environments. 'We build our brains through experience, both real and perceived', VELS tells us.** The ideal adult is to be one capable of a particular type of abstract thought, and not one connected to the spiritual realm. In VELS, the move to abstract knowing is a move towards uncertainty and flexibility. Having been developing their understanding of the adult social world already, the natural child is told as moving away from a belief in a singular and certain world. The overall framework, seeing 'students tend[ing] to progress from being concrete to abstract thinkers', is reminiscent of theories of the development of rationality. However, if abstract knowledge is about flexible and transferable patterns of knowledge, and about a comfort with uncertainty, speculation, and possibility, then the link between abstraction and rationality becomes interesting. The last sentence describing abstract

---

* Victorian Curriculum and Assessment Authority (2006): <http://vels.vcaa.vic.edu.au/ essential/ interdisciplinary/thinking/index.html> [accessed 10 October 2007]
** Victorian Curriculum and Assessment Author (2006): <http://vels.vcaa.vic.edu.au/stages/ yrsprepto4/index.html> [accessed 22 October 2007]

thinking is striking in this regard: abstract thinkers 'are more likely to have insights in random ways'.[*]

The 'natural child' of the Steiner school is to be kept separate from the adult social world, while the VELS 'natural child' is said to be always a part of that world. The Steiner child is to learn from their emotional and imaginative hearts, while the VELS child is to learn from the world by adding complexity to their neural networks. The Steiner child circles every seven years closer to the actual spiritual world and its abstract ways of thought. The VELS child climbs steps of increasing neural complexity. Whereas the 'natural child' of the Steiner vision is to move up to the spiritual realm, the 'natural child' of VELS is to move away from the sense that there is any singular realm.

## CONCLUSION: ETHICAL REPRESENTATION AND THE PROBLEM OF THE 'NORMAL'

Throughout the drafting process, I considered various ways of concluding this chapter. Most were negatively judgemental, trying to show through increasingly more sophisticated arguments that the imagination practised at this school was bad for children. Gradually though, I began to see that my ethical and analytic judgements were based on my own assumptions about what was normal or natural for children and education.

Practices at Steiner School clashed with my own unarticulated mental representation of the normal, including of the 'natural child'. I could make this child more explicit to myself, but except by beginning to 'see' the child as a Steiner teacher did, I could not avoid opposing Steiner practice. And I knew I could not honestly claim to be objectively representing. I seemed to have two choices: to agree or to disagree with Steiner representations of the 'natural child'. I would get only two options – Steiner schools are either good or bad. But of course things aren't so simple. The children in Shirley's classrooms were happy, friendly, and engaged in their learning. There is both good and bad here.

*   Victorian Curriculum and Assessment Authority (2006): <http://vels.vcaa.vic.edu.au/ essential/interdisciplinary/thinking/index.html> [accessed 10 October 2007]

One way out of the bind of thinking about representation in writing is to remember that when we write we are also intervening. (Hopefully) we change something in the ways readers can understand and act in the world. By telling about places where representations of the natural child clash and disturb, and also about the happy group of actual children in the Steiner classroom, perhaps we open some space for a mixing of the two ways of doing 'natural' children. Perhaps this looks as simple as having more storytelling in government classrooms, or as complex as a brain science-inflected Steiner programme. But, however it might happen, I hope that the intervention of making explicit might turn into the more significant intervention of hybridity.

**5**

# TELLING A GOOD YARN

*An Independent Classroom
and the Imagination that Transforms*

Mr Robertson is reading the spelling test, inventing a sentence to give context to each word. All are words that incorporate the 'ph' sound: dolphin, metaphor, graph, photo. Mr Robertson pretends the heavy accent of an Asian tourist, 'can I take your photo?' There is a rustle in the room as children look up, smiling. Mr Robertson turns to me, sitting at his desk with my notebook. He asks rhetorically, 'That was a bit racist, wasn't it?' I smile back. He turns back to the class and apologises. 'I wasn't putting down people with strong accents', he says.

They near the end of the test, and Grant puts up his hand and tells the class a funny story about how his little sister is always trying to get him into trouble. 'Do I promote chatting?' Mr Robertson asks me. It doesn't seem to worry him, for he continues, 'I don't want to be boring' (Independent School, author field notes, 20 April 2007).

MR ROBERTSON IS SEEN ABOVE TO FAVOUR A STYLE OF TEACHING AS A humorous performance. For his students he wants to display – and to model – the imagination of the entertainer. As the children laugh about his contextualisation of 'photo', he succeeds in transforming the list of spelling words into a comedy. Making Asian tourists into objects of fun, he himself becomes a 'person of fun'. Transforming the process of testing spelling, he finds he has also made the classroom into a scene for similar comic performances. These are bodily routines of imagination as performing for laughs. This requires imagination as creativity: the theme of this chapter. Throughout I will be arguing that imagination as creativity means performing transformations of self and other objects. I will illustrate this idea with examples taken from art and dramatic performance. To succeed, these performances need certain requirements, laid down by school, context, or materials worked with. Predominant among these requirements is discipline. Bodies and minds need to be disciplined in particular ways for creativity to succeed – or at least this is how imagination as creativity is practised in these primary schools.

I begin this chapter by looking at imagination as a creative *performance*, in particular one that should be humorous. We see this occur in a classroom at Independent School, and I go on to argue that certain features of this school explain the dominance there of this mode of imagination. In particular, I suggest that parental expectations that their children be transformed into 'self-actualising' individuals lead to a focus on ensuring that children appear to be creative individuals. Imagination at this school is used to solve a private problem: how to be a successful individual. To be successful at creative tasks requires that one also be technically skilful and disciplined. I show this through an examination of imagination as the creative *transformation* of self and objects, especially in art classes. This chapter then is about imagination practised as careful and creative performances that transform selves and objects.

## IMAGINATION AS CREATIVE PERFORMANCE: THE 'IMAGINEER'

Mr Robertson started his teaching career in the art room, having worked professionally as a potter before retraining to teach. He has now acted as the classroom teacher for various grades for more than fifteen years, all at this school. Mr Robertson describes himself as an 'imagineer', a term he borrows, or perhaps coins, to refer to the engineering of imagination. In thus explaining his teaching style and priorities, he suggests that he has the skill to engineer (to plan, oversee, or design) the imagination of children in his class. Imagination is a technical achievement. For Mr Robertson, imagination is, as he says, 'a good skill'. It is a particular talent, not associated with intelligence more broadly. 'Some children have it, but some children don't. Doesn't mean they're not intelligent or capable' (Independent School, author interview with teacher, 17 April 2007).

Teachers all around the school tell me that Mr Robertson is an imaginative teacher and expert at getting his children to do imaginative things. Their performances at school assemblies are mentioned in particular. Imagination, then, is a skill that Mr Robertson is considered to have himself as well as one he works to achieve in his children. The way 'imagination' is mobilised here is as skill in making products, whether these are imaginative children (Mr Robertson's job), or imaginative art works or drama pieces (children's jobs). In each of these cases, what is important is showing oneself as an imaginative person, noticeable as such because of the products or performances one crafts.

To be imaginative in this very particular way is to be successful in Mr Robertson's classroom. We see this in his interventions with a child who is deemed 'not imaginative'. Peter is often in trouble for being disruptive, not finishing work, and for being a 'know it all', especially about science and maths. He is not popular with the other children; at lunchtime he plays alone or goes to the library. Mr Robertson has worked to help this boy become more popular with his classmates by encouraging him to be more humorous. Mr Robertson's intent seems to be to help Peter transform himself and his role in the class by becoming a conscious entertainer. One morning, for example, Mr Robertson reads out the class's list of overdue library books. Peter is listed as having *Playschool* (a TV show for preschool children) still issued in his name. Mr Robertson reads this out, and the class starts to laugh. Peter whines, 'But I don't have it', and the class laughs some more. Mr Robertson addresses Peter. 'If you could learn to say,' he says, throwing his arms wide and singing the theme of the children's television show, 'open the door, it's playschool'. Mr Robertson goes on, 'if you could learn to say that then everyone would laugh with you. You've got to learn to diffuse the situation'. He begins to tell the class about what he did as a child when his brothers called him 'horse': he began neighing and pretending to gallop (Independent School, author field notes, 18 April 2007). Mr Robertson is advocating, and modelling, the self-transformation that should help Peter. Peter's role in the class will be transformed when he shows a creative imagination expressed as humorous performance in order to entertain the class. Mr

Robertson is trying, very explicitly, to be an imagineer by making Peter into an imaginative, humorous entertainer.

In this view, then, imagination is a creative performance. It is a performance that transforms the self into a creative self. Along the way, other objects may be transformed also. Let us explore this a little further.

## Performing Imagination: Role-plays

Role-plays are a technique used often with this class by Mr Robertson and by the various specialist teachers who work with them. By 'role-play' I mean the division of the class into small groups to discuss, develop, and perform a short play around a particular topic. Role-plays are intended to help children gain skills in group work, and in the planning and communication of ideas. What we see them gain also are the skills of planned and impromptu humour. In each episode of role-playing, we find children informally competing to get the biggest laugh out of their classmates and their teacher.

Humour is creative – children find ways to make contexts or ideas collide in unexpected or incongruous ways. Imagination is necessary here for making new links. But they are creative in a second sense too, as children compete to make themselves into the characters they play, and more, as many work to make themselves into the class clown. Creativity transforms the object it is performed through, even if that object is the creator. Role-plays, then, should be understood as a teaching technique that develops imaginative skills in con-necting and transforming selves. In being humorous, and with teachers' active encouragement, children link ideas and transform their fictive and social roles. They make themselves into and show themselves to be creative individuals.

An example:

> Mr Taylor, the physical education and health teacher, is taking a class about
> how to ask people not to smoke nearby. He splits the class into groups and
> gives each a scenario – someone smoking in a car; a public place; a home;
> in a friend group. The children begin to discuss and perform ideas in their
> groups. As they do so, I talk with Mr Taylor about the popularity of the

smoker role. We watch children fall to the floor in performances of exaggerated death. After spending time to decide what to present, the groups take turns. As each group performs, the laughter becomes louder and more frequent and the 'badness' of the 'smoker' (arguably) more marked. In the first, the smoker is also drinking and driving. In the second, the smoker forces a cigarette into the mouth of another customer at the pub. In the third, the smoker is a pregnant woman played by a boy, who spends the skit yelling at her child. In the final role-play, approval of smoking is performed by 'the devil' as a boy tries to decide whether to accept a cigarette from his friend (who dies loudly as soon as the offer has been made). Soon the devil dies too – having smoked not cigarettes but TNT. Across all these performances as the badness of smokers gradually escalates, class laughter increases, creating a feedback system encouraging students towards more humour. It is an unspoken competition: who can be the funniest and most creative, especially in the role of the smoker. Mr Taylor does not resist this trend, laughing as well but occasionally suggesting other, more restrained, ways to resolve the scenarios (Independent School, author field notes, 26 March 2007).

It is the same in the other role-plays I see performed at this school. These are numerous, occurring in library class, religious education, and in literacy classes with Mr Robertson. In all, it is the presentation of the humorous, imaginative self that is being achieved just as much as the presentation of the ideas the lesson is supposedly about.

This is not only true for Mr Robertson's grade four class. Rather, we see these performances validated by the school as a whole. Every Friday afternoon the school assembles in the large music room. This is a time for celebrating the achievement of students within and beyond the school. It is also a time for classes to perform for each other. Each week a class 'leads' the assembly, and their productions are designed to entertain. For example, a grade three class performs a published play called 'Mixed Up Rhymes'. They make most of the school laugh, children and adults alike. After the play is finished, they quiz the teachers on their knowledge of nursery rhymes, with child questioner and teacher respondent competing for laughs. 'Why did Humpty Dumpty break, Mr Wilsdon?' Mr

Wilsdon replies quickly and as if the answer is obvious, 'because he fell off the wall.' Droll, his child questioner adds, 'and because he was made out of eggs'. Mr Wilsdon and the audience laugh (Independent School, author field notes, 29 March 2007). The next week, the grade six class copy this assembly format, thereby acknowledging its success.

Independent School is not the only school to use humorous role-plays, but it is alone in employing them so frequently and with so little content beyond the presentation of children as humorous. At Catholic School, for example, a grade three/four class performs at assembly a humorous role-play they wrote themselves. Because it is nearly Father's Day, the children act out the relationship Jesus might have had with his father if both had been modern Australian 'blokes'. This too succeeds in making the audience laugh, but it is rich also in ideas. These are picked up and extended by the priest, who follows up the links made between Father's Day and God the Father. The children are encouraged here to understand the play's success as due to its treatment of serious issues, albeit in a humorous way (Catholic School, author field notes, 31 August).

So what is it about Independent School that makes role-plays so common? What can we discern about what it means to be successfully imaginative here? Answering this question will require a reminder that the meaning of 'creativity', and its relationship to 'imagination', vary cross-culturally and historically.

## IMAGINATION AS TRANSFORMATIVE: AUSTRALIA'S INDEPENDENT SCHOOLS

Mr Robertson teaches his class at an Anglican independent school, which, in Australia, means a private or fee-paying school. Fees are high here, restricting access to the children of wealthy homes. This allows class size to be kept low, and ensures that there are many active specialist programmes, including in the arts, sports, and technology. Why do parents choose to pay the high fees? What does the school promise and what do parents believe their children gain?

An independent market research study conducted in 1998 for the Association of Independent Schools of Victoria gives us some answers. By conducting and analysing twelve group discussions held around Australia, the authors of 'What

Parents Want from their Children's Education in Independent Schools' sought to answer their title in ways that would help independent schools design messages and media to attract client-parents.

The report's authors, Irving Saulwick and Denis Muller, concluded that despite diversity in socio-economic status and ethnicity, parents who choose independent schools share many aspirations for their children that go well beyond the economic. They point out that though this does not rule out 'traditional' interest in the 'three R's', in information-rich lessons, or discipline, the desires of parents now are quite different from those of the past. They report that most parents were members of the Australian middle class.

> They had imbibed its values. They were products of the post-industrial society. They, perhaps more than their own parents, had been brought up in a time when personal fulfilment was paramount, when self-actualisation, self-knowledge, self-development were seen as desirable and attainable goals. If this path led to a prosperous life, so much the better. But if it did not (and few imagined that it would lead to poverty) then for many the richness of personal fulfilment was to be preferred to the sterile life of economic security without joy (Saulwick and Muller, 2007: 3).

These findings are openly reflected in the prospectus handed out to parents upon visiting the school, at stalls at a schools exhibition and on the Internet. The prospectus for Independent School is a fourteen-page A4 book printed on thick glossy paper. Throughout there are photos of children wearing neat uniforms: for the girls pale blue dresses with Peter Pan collars, and for the boys white shirts, dark shorts, and pulled-up socks. Both girls and boys have the school crest on the left breast pocket. The children are shown playing games, playing sport, and playing music, or standing in groups. Always they are smiling (Gregory, undated). This booklet has been put up on the Internet, with software that lets you turn the pages with the cursor (Gregory 2007).

Handed out with the booklet was a DVD presenting life at the school under the headings 'Kinder' (as in kindergarten), 'Special Friends Day', 'Swimming', 'LOTE (Languages Other Than English) Day', 'Athletics', 'Chapel', 'Art', 'Music

Live', and 'Camp'. Over all scenes plays a medley of pop music, and what little speech there is comes from children. This mainly concerns why they like the school or explanations of what they are doing in the particular task filmed. In all, as they show work to grandparents, perform in orchestra and choir, present their art to the camera, or run in sack races, children are shown having serious fun. They are neat, polite, and above all, able to present themselves as cheerful, cute, and well behaved (Glowworm productions, undated). They perform themselves as having been transformed by the school into creative, happy, and disciplined individuals.

Mr Robertson and the other teachers at this school have a dual challenge. They must teach the children the knowledge and skills expected by parents and state; and they must ensure that the children become, and show themselves to have become, self-actualising, and personally fulfilled. They must be evidently happy, active individuals, and always in the process of becoming even more so, of reaching towards their potential. They are to do this by performing a particular version of imagination as creativity.

## CREATIVITY

### Creativity and Re-Imagining Imagination

Creativity and imagination are closely related concepts. This has been repeatedly brought to my attention as people refer to children's art and craft when I tell them that I am studying imagination at primary school: *imagination is creativity is art*, the logic seems to run. But the exact nature of their relationship is not only hard to pin down; it is also ever-changing. Questions we need to ask are multiple, and referred to tangentially below. They include: should we speak of people as imaginative and products creative? (Briskman 1981). Or can people sensibly be referred to as creative? If so, does a person become more 'creative' as they make creative things? (Krausz 1981). What should a teacher's role be – to teach children the technical skills they need to make creative products or to teach a process of creativity itself? (Khatena 1999; Sak 2004). Should teachers assess the 'creativity' or 'imagination' of their students, and if so, how? (Feldman 1994; Ward 2004).

Answers to these questions vary across places and times. As has been shown in Kaufman and Sternberg's 2006 edited volume *The International Handbook of Creativity*, definitions of what creativity is and how important it should be for knowledge, technology, and the nation-state vary from culture to culture. Variations appear to be caused by diverse factors, such as whether individualism or collective forms of life are considered more natural; whether people are encouraged to aim for the new or continue to follow tradition; how challenge is regarded; and what value is put on education. These cultural factors underpin systems of education as well as the economic systems in which new creative products are deemed valuable (Stenberg 2006). Understanding the relation between imagination and creativity, and the relative and absolute values placed upon each, requires an understanding of a culture and its systemic forms of life.

We also need to recognise that these values change over time. With them change definitions of imagination and creativity as concepts relative to each other and absolute. Meyer Abrams made this point in his 1953 *The Mirror and the Lamp*. In this study of literary creativity, he argued that whereas imagination in the classical and early modern era was spoken of as the reflection of another reality, the mark of the Romantic era was the transformation of imagination to mean the generation of light into the mysteries of human emotion. New forms of creative writing were produced; for example, those of Wordsworth and Coleridge that have been understood as turning points in the modern imagination (Warnock 1976; White 1990). Richard Kearney, adding to this model in 1991, suggested that modern and post-modern imagination could best be likened to a 'labyrinth of looking glasses', the creation, refraction, and illusion of multiple, self-referential objects (Pope 2005: 14–17).

## Creativity and Becoming

While imagination and creativity are distinct and varying, both imagination and creativity can be usefully understood as processes of transformation. This can be the transformation of ideas, materials, or selves.

In 1967, Arthur Koestler first published a paper entitled 'The Three Domains of Creativity' in which he tried to establish that creative thinking in scientific discovery, artistic originality, and comic inspiration were part of one underlying system. What all have in common, for Koestler, was that all are ways of joining pieces of previously known information in new ways. All are new ways of performing information in the mind and in the world. They are moments of epiphany marked by verbal and physical responses. Scientific discovery he describes as the merging of two or more pieces of information or forms of logic previously kept separate. Humour, by contrast, is the collision of information or logic systems. As Koestler put it, 'Comic discovery is paradox stated – scientific discovery is paradox resolved' (Koestler 1981: 3). Artistic originality completes the continuum, with the sublime artist successfully juxtaposing pieces of information or logic, creating a work that transcends the meaning of either lone piece.

Koestler's piece is just as much about the effects these forms of creativity have on those who experience them as either creator or observer: reactions that he calls Aha (for science), haha (for humour), and ah (for art). 'The Haha reaction signals the collision of bisociated contexts; the Aha reaction signals their fusion; and the Ah reaction signals their juxtaposition' (Koestler 1981:10). Different creative combinations of information or logic can produce involuntary responses ranging from surprised laughter, through the shout 'eureka', to self-transcending sighs of appreciation.

Such an elegant system is obviously reductive, bringing the complexity of creative moments and the multiplicity of types of creativity into a typology referring to one common feature – that each is a way of combining. The materiality of this transforming imagination is obvious in the case of art, where an artist combines materials to create new pieces. Writers likewise transform by combining, although their material is language. Both seek to express new meanings through their combinations (see also Vygotsky (1930): 2004: 7–97).

This capacity is not limited to artists, but can be generalised to all humans as they speak. This is the argument that Ronald Carter makes, claiming that all people display creativity as they engage in talk: '[L]inguistic creativity is not simply a property of exceptional people but an exceptional property of all people'. Throughout his book, *Language and Creativity: The Art of Common Talk*, Carter uses extended extracts of conversation to show how individual and group identity is extended and transformed as topics and word patterns, and meanings are passed around speakers. By using language, people transform their relationships, and those speakers are, likewise, transformed (Carter 2004).

## Creativity as Extension

We have seen that Independent School promises parents that their children will be transformed by their time here into self-actualising and fulfilled children. This will be achieved, in large part, by ensuring that the children are able to perform themselves as creative individuals who are able to transform the world (albeit in small ways). Children must be seen to be happily creative. This is achieved through humorous performances of the self, as we have seen. Another key site for showing oneself to be creative is the art room. But there is a challenge: how to balance the creative impulse with the need for technical skill. This we will turn to soon with the concept of the disciplined creative imagination, but first let us think a little about the relationship between creativity and developing the potential self. For this, we turn to two thinkers on art.

Philosopher Michael Krausz and anthropologist Alfred Gell had a similar interest in the relationship between art and the development of selves. For both, the closeness of this relationship calls into fundamental question the dualism of subject and object. For both, artistic creativity is a process of becoming more than a subject, more than oneself.

For Krausz this insight comes from his own experience of making art, particularly the moments of what he calls 'at-one-ness' with the work being crafted (Krausz 1981:195). This indicates to him that the process of making art is a process of transcending the self, of being joined somehow to the art object. The transformation of the self is not incidental here, but fundamental to art itself. He says, 'if one circumscribes as one's artwork the production of art objects and one's self-development in a mutually enriching complex, then the objectivist rejection of subjective considerations as part and parcel of a work of art cannot be maintained' (Krausz 1981: 191). By making art one transforms oneself.

For Gell too, art enables becoming more than the self in a process he describes as 'extended agency'. To make this argument, Gell distinguishes between primary (or intentional) agents and secondary agents. If primary agents are people or things that can intentionally cause events, then secondary agents are those persons or objects through which agency is conducted. The power and reach of one's agency can be extended via art objects, again making the process of creativity a process of becoming bigger than the self. He makes this argument through reference to examples gathered during a life of anthropological research (Gell 1998).

So for both Krausz and Gell, art is the concretisation of one's body-transcendent self in the art object. Those objects might then exert some power in the world. With the practice of the creative imagination, humans might transform their subject positions to actualise their potential to be more than they were. In theory, artistic creativity is transformative of the self.

But what about in practice? We might expect that art classes are an ideal place to see the transformative element of creative imagination in action. However, what we learn by looking at art classes is that other skills must be laid down first. Art classes give us a glimpse of teachers *resisting* the creative imagination in favour of the skills they take to be necessary for its later expression. Revealed is a set of necessary conditions for the achievement of creative imagination in art classes, where technical skill is seen as more important than, and a basis for, creative work. This is about disciplined control over transformations of self and object.

## DISCIPLINED SELVES, CREATIVE SELVES

Art is always some combination of technical skill and creativity. The technical is inherent in it being an embodied and usually materially mediated activity, while the creative is part of art by definition – what is only technical would not be called properly artistic. These two sides of art, the technical and creative, map onto two ways of thinking about imagination. Imagining in art takes on two meanings, one relating to the skill of visualising objects and the other relating to creativity. So the question in this section becomes: how do teachers in their particular school context balance technical and creative skills? The answers, we will find, all involve a new figure – the disciplined imagination. This is necessary for the creative transformation of materials to succeed.

Again, we start with Independent School.

I think that Mr Jarvis, the art teacher, has made a joke and I laugh. He's just said, 'imagination? I try to stamp it out of them'. I realise he wasn't joking later that day when Mr Robertson's class has art. Mr Jarvis explains to them that their next project is self-portraits, and he shows some prints by famous artists. Their own self-portraits will be marked on two criteria; how smooth the colour change is in their shading, and how accurately they have the proportions according to a formula he teaches in stages throughout class time. By taking this lesson seriously, he tells them, they will find that they master the difficult skills of art, and these are not imaginative. 'Making things up is too easy. Sometimes to be a good artist you have to know how to copy' (Independent School, author field notes, 27 March 2007).

For this art teacher, the drive towards developing technical skills makes unnecessary even imagination as visualising objects. Copying correctly is a source of skill and of ideas.

Mr Jarvis also runs an art club one lunchtime per week. Too many children wanted to attend than could be accommodated, so classroom teachers choose children on the grounds of their skill, the number of other extra-curricular activities taken, and whether it would be 'good' for them in a psychological sense. For various reasons these are children deemed to need more opportunities for self-actualisation and personal fulfilment. In art club, they are to draw animals, gradually developing ideas through the term before painting a canvas to take home. Mr Jarvis instructs them to bring a picture the following week of the animal they want to draw. One girl asks, 'does it have to be a real animal?' and suggests a unicorn. She is told that would be fine so long as she has a picture of a unicorn to copy: 'It can't be an animal just in your head because we need things to draw' (Independent School, author field notes, 16 April 2007). Ideas for these art classes should not come from minds, but from the trial and error of increasingly skilled hands as they physically copy real pictures.

Disciplined technical skill is seen here to be a necessary condition for creativity in art. But discipline is important in ensuring the success of creative imagination more generally. The disciplining of bodies and minds is necessary for the transformation of selves into creative selves.

## Silence and Sound: Disciplining Imaginative Minds for Transformation

> Mrs Rich comes back after the class has spent an hour with a relief teacher,
> and finds them unsettled. She asks them to close their books and their eyes,
> and 'think of something you find peaceful [...] Let's think about the things
> we think of when I say the word "peace".' She gives them ideas – a peaceful
> place in the playground, people in our class, or in their family, who make
> them feel peaceful. The class becomes calm and Mrs Rich begins her next
> lesson (Catholic School, author field notes, 10 September 2007).

What Mrs Rich does is transform minds into spaces of peace so that the behaviours of bodies, vocal chords, and thinking minds might change.

Without some discipline, creative tasks do not succeed. Whereas Cropley argues that teachers discipline children to discourage the personality traits linked with creativity (such as impulsiveness, non-conformity and disorganisation) (1992: 18–19), I suggest that teachers discipline to make creative moments possible (see also Sak 2004).

Certain ways of disciplining minds and bodies are required by teachers for the production of imaginative moods. This can mean the type of discipline required for classroom management. The room must be filled with a reasonable quantity of sound. Teachers will often insist on silence while creative work is being done. Government School teacher Justine expresses this when she claps her hands for attention while her class write creative stories. She asks the class, 'what do writers need?' and answers herself: 'special uninterrupted quiet' (Government School, author field notes, 21 May 2007). Here the quiet Justine insists on is to have a 'special' aspect to it, in keeping with the special nature of creative work. This quiet is necessary to let minds become poised on the cusp of creative thought, and to sometimes slip over.

Minds are to be disciplined into imaginative moods not only with silence but also with particular sounds. Music is regarded as powerful in this regard. The art teacher at Government School always plays classical music before starting her classes, because, as Bridget reminds the class when asked, 'it takes our brains to the creative side'. When the Mozart piece is finished the teacher asks

Sally to identify someone who 'was being very relaxed but also very tuned in'. She suggests to her class that concentrated relaxation is the ideal bodily state for imagination and creativity (Government School, author field notes, 24 May 2007).

The disciplining of bodies and sounds together also produces creative moods. With silence and stillness, imaginative moods are made possible. This becomes palpable during Mrs Rich's Friday afternoon drama class, the last class of the week and a time for relaxation, imagination, and fun. However, this is not to come at the expense of discipline, but rather requires discipline. During one drama session, the class plays a game in which they have to picture a scene in their heads they can photograph. When chosen, they move other children into the positions required. Those children are not to move from their positions, making the group into a still 'photo'. Mrs Rich demonstrates, moving children into a pose. There are giggles and distraction, and she warns, 'Drama is a time for fun; it's not a time for silliness. I think we'll stop'. After a pause for children to show they are quiet, she completes the scene, mimes taking a photo, and lets the children guess what the scene shows – a wedding. Now it is the children's turn and they are to position people without speaking (Catholic School, author field notes, 31 August 2007). Click, and an imaginary photo of children transformed.

## CONCLUSION: SPINNING A GOOD YARN

Mr Robertson says that the art of teaching is 'spinning a good yarn'. Throughout this chapter, I have tried to argue the significance of the yarns he spins are, partly, that they enable Mr Robertson to present imagination as a particular type of skill. This skill is amenable to 'engineering', as Mr Robertson puts it. In his manner of telling stories, he models the ability of imagination to transform oneself into an entertaining performer. Children practise these skills as they perform humorous role-plays in class and assembly times. These various performances not only show the creative skill of linking information but also as transforming self and world.

But creative transformations are not straightforward, and nor do they occur necessarily in the places we would expect. Discipline and the development of technical skill are necessary conditions for a creative imagination to be successfully engineered. Teachers work hard to balance imagination and discipline during art and drama classes. By keeping such discipline, teachers help their children to become capable of art and performances that better embody their imaginative ideas. Disciplined minds and bodies, as well as imaginative ones, are necessary for the achievement of creative moments. It takes a combination of imagination and control to make the creative links that successfully transform selves and objects, that extend agency, and that call up the moments of aha, haha, and ah.

**6**

# THINKING OF OTHERNESS

*A Government Classroom and Reading Intention*

The teacher, Justine, has written the timetable on the whiteboard. First, at 9am, is mathematics, then, at 10am, literacy. Next is a break, and after that, it's topic work. She has planned this day, and all the days of the week, and the term: she has decided, following school goals and curriculum, how to divide her school days to ensure children reach certain learning outcomes. Moreover, as she divides the class into groups for this morning's mathematics and gives out work sheets and other tasks, she has goals for what her children will gain from this hour, from 9am to 10am. This is to say that she has intentions for the learning of others. They are intentions she writes into her lesson plans as firm, clear, and achievable. This is her job.

Today it is windy outside, and a Friday morning, and several of the kids are out of sorts and misbehaving. One keeps talking while the teacher does. Another has had their seat taken and is crying. The teacher Justine is very sensitive to these types of problems and spends a long time talking through techniques for dealing with the upsets of life. We start mathematics late, and some children don't settle into work, continuing instead to be silly (Government School, author field notes, 24 May 2007).

JUSTINE KNOWS AS SHE WRITES HER LESSON PLANS THAT THESE DAYS HAPPEN sometimes, that her intentions can be derailed, but that, if she is flexible, other lessons are learnt instead. She knows pragmatically about the patterns of children's resistance to her plans and the accommodations she must make in the course of the day. This is similar to what Michael Pickering refers to as 'the mangle of practice' (Pickering 1994).*

This chapter is about one issue that gets caught up in the negotiation of lessons between children and teacher, between sure plans and changing needs. That issue is the taking of new perspectives. This is what Justine takes imagination to be: 'opening your mind up to other possibilities and seeing things differently, just drawing on ideas and experiences [for] imagining putting yourself into a different time, a different space' (Government School, author interview with teacher, 29 May 2007). The chapter comes in two parts. In the first, I tell a story about the achievement of this imagination which is supposed to meet the requirements of a certain type of politics. This is to talk of the routines that teach perspective-taking as empathy, and places this in terms of the culturally sensitive politics of a multicultural nation-state. By empathy I mean the ability to 'see into' the life of another, to see with their eyes. This is a reading of imagination as a tool for achieving a 'good' form of civic education and thus as a solution to a public problem. Imagination as empathy teaches children to respect and understand other cultures, backgrounds, and habits. In this section, I tell of a teacher working hard to embed routines of empathy in the children she teaches, and I suggest lines of critique.

But as I have hinted above, and will develop in the second section of this chapter, things are not so simple. Justine does intend to impart skills in empathising to her students. But she also intends to respond to students' needs and sometimes these intentions clash. A skilled teacher, like Justine whom I discuss in this chapter, is skilled partly because she is comfortable negotiating between her intentions for learning and the ways lessons just end up going due to the unpredictable needs and interests of children. This is a skill in picking up and

---

* I say similar because Pickering's concept is designed for the relationship between human agency and material agency, whereas I am interested in the relationship between the intention exercised in practice by human agents with different degrees of power in the context of the classroom. Pickering and I are both interested in intention. The difference between human and material agents, as Pickering sees it, is that human agents have intention: 'we humans live in time in a particular way. We construct goals that refer to presently nonexistent future states and then seek to bring them about. I can see no reason to suppose that DNA double helices or televisions organize their existence thus — why should they?' (Pickering 1994: 565–566).

following chance remarks, or tears, or the conflicts that occurred at lunchtime, and turning these into useful lessons. Her interventions are good because they are responses to the ongoing passages in her classroom. What is the result? Adequately answering this question requires acknowledging the impact the messiness of practice has on a participant-observer.

I too had intentions about what I wanted to see. Justine talked about empathy; I knew it was a good of her lessons. I had read and thought a lot about empathy in education (Macknight 2007; 2008; 2010) and I lived in a nation-state where empathy is part of good politics. All these things made me want to interpret the moments of perspective-taking I experienced in this classroom as successful or less successful performances of teaching empathy. This was my intention – but the contingencies of practice resisted so simple an interpretation. Now instead I have revised my intention and I write about the broader concept of perspective-taking.

Making this move is part of trying to be a participant-observer who recognises that they are part of what they later write about. This is part of the move away from telling about classrooms through modes of representation. I seek here to tell of my ways of responding to the events that I witnessed, both at the time and retrospectively. To that end, in the two parts of this chapter I present myself as two types of witness: one, a witness who observes and represents the facts about what happened (one who thinks she is observing from an impartial distance) and the second, a more corporeal and emotional witness (who recognises her situated and emotional body). Doing so reminds us of Donna Haraway's figure of the 'modest witness' (1997). She is a figure who can tell a different kind of story, and it is one I appeal to here. Crucially, she is a witness who does not aim for a single explanation.

The argument I make in this chapter, then, is that a good witness is comfortable with more than one interpretive lens. She does not see classroom practices succeeding or not in terms of a single intention stated by a teacher, but in regard to how the teacher negotiates between her intentions and those of others, and how she brings alive broader and richer versions of her plans. In this case, I argue that instead of 'empathy' we should talk about perspective-taking. Extending the metaphors of perspective-taking as 'seeing into' and 'seeing from' that I introduce in the first part of this chapter, I suggest two alternative ways we might talk about perspective-taking – 'seeing with' and 'seeing for'. Justine's intention might be to teach imagination as empathy, but it is also to teach these other ways of taking another's perspective. Realising that it was my intention, my hope, to see and write about practices of imagination as empathy enables a richer reading of classroom practice. The result, I argue, is a new way to understand the complexity of intention involved in teaching imagination and an expanded politics of civic education.

## EMPATHY

### 'Could you Imagine Being Him?'

We gather in the biggest classroom, and all the school's grade three and four children find spaces to sit cross-legged on the floor. They crane their heads up to look at the 'special guest'. He is very tall, very black, and has spent most of his twenty-odd years in exile. This is what he tells about today, starting from fleeing Eritrea with his family to a refugee camp in Sudan. He details material aspects of life there, comparing these to how he assumes these school children live: cooking on fires, not stoves; no books, no libraries, no schools; nothing to do but play soccer if male, and cook if female. His story continues. He escaped the refugee camp for Saudi Arabia, advancing from there to Egypt and thence, finally, to a nearby Melbourne suburb, here, in Australia.

The children listen, as the teachers stand watching them, ready to shush whispers and still restless limbs. Now as he finishes his story, the teachers come back to life, with one telling the assembled children that it is time to ask questions. The keenest children put their hands up, looking from teacher to guest for permission to speak. Pointing, the guest calls on child after child.

Most questions come direct from the interview sheets the children had taken home and used to glean a migration story from a family member. These sheets had originally been given out as homework, acceptable as such because they were deemed to constitute a piece of 'authentic learning', something embedded in the lives of the children. When, earlier that week, Justine's class had another 'special guest', Justine had held this sheet up and suggested the classes' questions should come from it.

So now, the children ask the questions teachers wrote for them to ask their families.

Some questions are generic and have already been included in the guest's story. 'Where did you first live in Australia?' 'I lived in Flemington', he says, patient though he's already told them.

Other questions might enable rich replies if asked of older migrants, but for this life story are confusing. 'Did you have any difficulties during your travel to Australia?' No, he tells them, catching a plane was very easy and comfortable.

Most questions forget that this was a story of fleeing war. These are answered quickly. 'What possessions do you still have from your home?' None. 'Do you wish you hadn't decided to leave?' No. One boy asks, 'Were you ever shot?', and the teacher says, hurriedly, 'Next question'.

We walk back to our particular classrooms, and sit again on the mat. 'Could you imagine being him?' Justine asks. 'Imagine what it must have been like!' (Government School, author field notes, 22 May 2007)

These children are being taught a set of routines that involve looking, listening, and questioning with the intent of helping them see into the perspective of another person, imagining what it must have been like. Given 'perspective resources' in the form of guests, picture and chapter books, timelines, biographies, and classmates, they are taught a set of questions to ask of them. There are particular skills involved in asking questions well, and these children have not yet all absorbed them. Some have not listened closely enough; others have not had the experience with objects, like planes, to ask interesting questions. These are signs that the children are still learning the complex of listening and thinking skills that make these perspective-taking routines work smoothly. Moreover, they have not all learnt a more socially significant set of rules, those that govern what is an appropriate question in this community. To be a good questioner is to avoid upsetting people; it is to ask things that make our interlocutors like us (having migrated, travelled, having special processions, deciding things) not unlike us (shooting, being shot at, running away).

Through the material technology of questions printed on pieces of paper, practised in several situations and increasingly without the paper itself, these children are learning to speak a set of accepted questions. And, through glaring at and telling off children who ask questions deemed inappropriate, another set of standards come into play – those governing acceptable questions in civic life. The teacher rounds off by requesting that children imagine what it would have been like to be the guest. This appears to encapsulate the lesson as having been about perspective-taking as empathy: imagining oneself in the life of another.

So, what I initially believed I had witnessed in this (and other) lessons at this school was the teaching of routines that embed routines of imagination as empathy in children. The notion of empathy as a kind of 'seeing into' the world or perspectives of another person, time, or place has a long history.

## Empathy and 'Seeing Into'

Analyses of empathy began in embryonic form with Giovanni Vico, according to Isaiah Berlin, and grew with Herder. Vico's great insight, in his 1725 *New Science*, was to see that myths were human articulations of experience. In thinking our way bodily into these myths, through the method of 'recollective fantasia' we could come to understand past human experience. We would be able to 'see into' the life of another. The tool for the human project of self-understanding would be the logic of imagination (Berlin 1976; Verene 1981; Vico 2002).

Isaiah Berlin ties the insights of Vico and Herder to map broader intellectual trends. According to Berlin, these two figures can be read as opponents of the Enlightenment notions that were slowly taking hold. Where Enlightenment figures said that humans were all essentially the same, counter-Enlightenment thinkers said that culture makes us different. Where Enlightenment figures believed in the logic of science, induction, and laws for knowing about other cultures, the counter-Enlightenment thinkers believed in the need for poetry, art, and imagination to get glimpses of otherness (Berlin 1976).

These are also a politics, one that has been a basic part of nation-states' dealings with 'culture', albeit in radically divergent ways. Commonly, arguments for the intrinsic difference and value of culture to specific groups have been used to justify a politics of multiculturalism. In a piece of previous work, I found an example of this politics. Looking at the curriculum and reading resources of Victorian primary schools in the 1930s, I was struck by the many lessons, stories, articles, and photos that were published in an explicit attempt to show that 'children in other lands' were not really so different from those in Australia. If children could see into the world as experienced by the differently acculturated children in other lands, then they could sympathise and feel affection for them. By these means, future wars might be avoided (Macknight 2007; 2008).

Meanwhile however, the conviction that cultural difference causes us to experience the world differently can also be used as argument for the radial incommensurability of cultures. This understanding of cultural difference was the basis of the post-1918 division of Europe into ethnically defined nation-states. Each ethnic group was to be self-governing and by this means civil (and other wars) would be avoided. These ideas were called into Nazi and neo-Nazi ideology (see, Holmes 2000). If everyone really was so different, some must be better than others and some worse. For obvious reasons, we tend to avoid the notion of radical incommensurability and settle instead for a level of difference that can be imagined into via empathy.

So influential has the notion of empathy become that Currie and Ravenscroft argue that empathy and thinking into the worlds of others is usually what people mean by the term 'imagination'. To recreate the lives of others, 'to project ourselves into another situation and to see, or think about, the world from another perspective', they claim is the folk meaning of imagination (Currie and Ravenscroft 2002: 1). Though I have not met this meaning often in my dealing with 'the folk' (whoever they are), it does permeate education literature, again as a type of politics. Maxine Greene, for example, discusses what she calls 'social imagination'. This is intended as part of the achievement of a political goal of education – making better communities through better ways of knowing 'others'. Her Marxist leanings are clear. For her, the goal of education should be to teach social critique that 'entails an ongoing effort to overcome false consciousness by rejecting an absolute and state view of reality' (Greene 1995: 61). To achieve this she advocates a process whereby dialogue between diverse people is made meaningful by empathy. In Greene's words, we (including children) should learn to 'look in some manner through strangers' eyes and hear through their ears' and therefore 'cross the empty spaces between ourselves and those we have called "other"' (Greene 1995: 3).

Imagination as empathy has also been assumed to be vital to good history education. David Stockley, for example, following an article by Boddington, argued that successful history lessons would be those that produced empathy in students. This he defined as stepping into others' minds to gain an understanding of motives and actions and a vicarious experience of humanity within a historical frame of reference. This was not to be confused with sympathy because this would not be an appropriate emotion to feel for most historical agents. And, he was careful to add, this was imagination – by which he meant that it would be formed of a mixture of knowledge and emotion: 'Empathetic reconstruction combines analytical and emotional skills and requires substantial contextual knowledge' (Stockley 1983: 60).

## Empathy as an Everyday Political Goal

There have recently been significant changes in how perspective-taking is understood in the Victorian curriculum. There has been a move away from empathy across cultural boundaries replaced by a stress on improving children's skills in talking and working with people from other cultures. This is a politics that replaces the uniqueness of cultural others with a politics of getting along.

Empathy remains, however, a notion widely expressed in the primary school classrooms I visited and by their teachers. A few examples:

- the first in a row of posters displayed above the whiteboard in the class at Government School reads, 'Listening and Understanding with

Empathy – Understand Others! – Devoting mental energy to another person's thoughts and ideas; holding in abeyance one's own [...]' (Government School, author field notes, 22 May 2007);

- of her teaching, Mrs Rich explains during our interview that 'Dealing with the children I teach, I imagine what their life must be like at home. So I s'pose I'm constantly thinking, imagining, putting myself in others shoes, in many areas' (Catholic School, author interview with teacher, 11 September 2007); and

- telling about what he believes mainstream schools should learn from the Steiner approach assistant teacher Paul says, 'I think that ability to put yourself in someone else's shoes, and that's something that's lacking a lot in our society' (Steiner School, author interview with teacher, 15 June 2007).

These words, collected from a bigger corpus of like examples, reveal that empathy remains an important goal for primary school teachers. It is simultaneously intended to guide children into better understandings of others, to be a tool to help teaching, and as a step towards the goal of improving society.

Given that empathy is a goal for primary school teachers, there are important questions to ask about whether they achieve it in their students. We can work in a sceptical mood, pointing out as I did after the opening story where empathy is stopped or where it misrepresents perspectives. By only focusing on some features of life in camps, and planes, and new countries, children are encouraged only to see into certain aspects of the refugee's life. Likewise, to give an example from a history lesson, by describing the physical experience of sleeping in a mid-nineteenth century goldfields shanty, children are helped only to imagine themselves in that past, rather than understand that this might have seemed different to those nineteenth century men and women who did sleep there. This is to suggest that 'seeing into' is an inappropriate aim for it encourages us to focus on what is familiar, not the great realms of mystery contained in other people and other times. As Samuel Weinburg puts it, 'the goal of historical study should be to teach us what we *cannot* see, to acquaint us with the congenital blurriness of our vision' (Weinburg 2001:11).

Furthermore, beyond the epistemological problem that 'seeing into' might produce incomplete or inaccurate knowledge, it also encourages what Lorraine Code identifies as a dangerous ethics. By assuming that others are essentially like us, we claim that 'I know just how you feel'. These claims might, however, be beset by issues of power and a belief in one's own authority to know. Such claims might be closer to the statement 'I know just how I would feel if I were in your situation' and may stop us from really listening to others. When we recall that much supposed empathy work is done by professionals in medical and state bureaucracies, this becomes a danger to those poor, sick, or otherwise needy people subject to their 'empathy' (Code 1995, especially pp. 120–143).

Important though they certainly are, critiques of this nature are not what I am interested in providing here. Instead, I want to explore the assumptions that lie behind a reading of Justine's perspective-taking routines as empathy, or better, as only empathy. To do so, we turn to an inquiry into the nature of my own witnessing. We ask about the complex play of intentions, resistances, and accommodations performed by children, teacher, and myself. This takes us first back to the classroom that I described at the start of this chapter.

## A CRITIQUE OF YOUR WITNESS — 'SEEING FROM'

These events happened at Government School located in the middle-class inner suburbs of Melbourne. I told something of this classroom in chapter one; of its school context and my happiness there. I said that often riding home I would feel actively happy, soothed, and validated in some deep way. Let me say more about the multiple nature of class in this particular site in order to cast suspicion on my initial readings of what these imaginative routines were about. This will show the classroom embedded in a wider community of practice that takes as basic and natural what Erica Burman (1994) has seen as the production of white middle-class notions of 'normal' child development.

First, and simply, this class was a unit of a school located in, and drawing children from, an area of modest affluence a short distance from the city centre. The median weekly family income in this neighbourhood is well above that of Australia as a whole ($1,636 compared to $1,171 according to the 2006

Australian census) (Australian Bureau of Statistics, 2008). Financially then, these children likely come from middle class homes.

Moreover, this government school works to attract parents with a particular view of the role of schools in society. Governments should pay for educating children, either because it is 'right' in political terms or, in the case of parents who could not choose otherwise, is necessary. These are notions of the state's role inherited from welfare state politics. What this school takes as its role is articulated in more detail in the material given to new parents. It is to produce naturally social children. The Government School parents' book has a glossy cover showing children playing, reading, and doing schoolwork. The central photo is of a girl, with a big gappy smile, her hair blowing across her face. These children are messy and childlike, but happy. The text inside emphasises 'authenticity' and a natural happy environment (Hilton and Malmgren undated).

In practice, 'authenticity' is a frame for the routines that discipline children towards good behaviour. They are routines of mutual responsibility, based on the idea that others' feelings are like one's own. When a child complains she has been left out of a game of cops and robbers, Justine asks the culprits, 'Can you see that Daniel would have felt like that? Would you have felt like that?' Acknowledgement that they would have is taken to be lesson enough on how to behave: if you would feel left out and upset, so will others (Government School, author field notes, 28 May 2007). This policy is explained to me as natural in our world of social conventions. This is a world in which all are expected to behave equally well, regardless of a person's superior or inferior power. The physical education teacher tells it in these terms: 'It just makes sense, it's how you live in the world, you know, if you drive a car it's your responsibility to drive it according to the rules' (Government School, author field notes, 30 May 2007). This school takes 'seeing into' to be both a vital and a relatively simple procedure. Others are presumed just as naturally social as oneself. This is how society runs.

In telling about this class and this school in this way – as representing a politics – I do a particular type of witnessing. This type of witnessing constructs me as a reliable observer and reporter of events and the ideas behind them.

However, the suggestion I have been making throughout this book (and in chapter one in particular) is that we should learn to see classrooms as both 'representatives of' and 'ongoing processes in'. This can be drawn into Donna Haraway's discussion of the witness.

Haraway gives us the figure of the modest witness set both with and against the witness of Enlightenment empiricism. The Enlightenment witness is the rational observer and recorder of the facts of the world as they are reflected off objects and into his retina. This witnessing is powerful, and provides power to those who are entitled to use it. They have been gifted 'the elaborately constructed and defended confidence of this civic man of reason' (Haraway 1997: 24). This witness wants to, and can, say definitively that this explains that.

Haraway's modest witness, just like her less modest cousin, does care about and attest to matters of fact. But she does so in ways that do not rely only on reflection. She is a 'more corporeal, inflected, and optically dense, if less elegant, kind of modest witness to matters of fact' (Haraway 1997: 24). As such, she might see in diffraction patterns instead of, or as well as, by reflection. Haraway explains the physics behind her diffraction metaphor:

> when light passes through slits, the light rays that pass through are broken up. And if you have a screen at one end to register what happens, what you get is a record of the passage of the light rays onto the screen. This 'record' shows the history of their passage through the slits. So what you get is not a reflection; it's the record of a passage. [ ... ] It's simply to make visible all those things that have been lost in an object; not in order to make the other meanings disappear, but rather to make it impossible for the bottom line to be one single statement (2000: 103 and 105).

A modest witness, then, might see depth and complexity within the facts. She might accept her sensitive body as integral to her acts of witnessing. She might say this is a record of working towards this *and* that.

With this modest witness in mind, here is the greater analytic significance of the class story I have just told. I myself attended government schools, sent by parents with the middle-class political morals likely to assume the 'good' of empathy. I attended a university at the time when curriculum documents that stressed empathy were being written and enforced (Curriculum Standards Framework One (1995) and Two (2000)), a time when the problems of globalisation and diversity were understood and solved through the discourse of multiculturalism and its companion empathy. This is where I was 'seeing from', but I could learn to see in a new, more modest, way.

These facts about my classed and classing body make me suspect as an Enlightenment witness, or more obviously suspect than most. Being admittedly corporeal, my ability to rationally observe is compromised. What your witness feels is the tug of familiarity in this place and in these ways of becoming a good citizen, and also the validation of a deeply felt ethical programme. What comes to be reflected most strongly into her retina is the object she already expects and wants to see – that of imagination as empathy. From the start of the ethics process, to justify her project in terms of empathy, she wrote that she intended to study how teachers imparted imagination as empathy to their students. And look, she found it!

However, if we see as modest witnesses, empathy is not the only object that we could distinguish in teachers' complex routines of perspective-taking. Looking through the diffracting slits we can also see at least two more types of perspective-taking being performed. Looking in this way also enables us to write in terms of Pickering's notion of the 'mangle of practice'. This is a dialectic process, formed in the relation of material (or, in this case, human) resistance and the intending human agents' accommodation to those resistances over time. This is a process of modifying intention and subsequent practice. He explains: '"Mangle" here is a convenient and suggestive shorthand for the dialectic: for me, it conjures up the image of the unpredictable transformations worked upon whatever gets fed into the old-fashioned device of the same name used to squeeze the water out of washing' (Pickering 1994: 567). Despite teacher intentions for empathy, she assesses other forms of perspective-taking as being successful even when children mangle her intentions. I call these 'seeing with' and 'seeing for', and they are articulated by Helen Verran and by Government School teacher Justine respectively.

## TWO NEW WAYS OF SEEING PERSPECTIVE-TAKING
### 'Seeing With'

Here is another story of what happened in Justine's classroom that was initially interesting to me because it seemed a failed attempt to teach perspective-taking as empathy.

> The kids are polite, but bored. We have a special guest here today, sitting up the front with Justine. An old woman, who needs help standing up from her chair but who still goes dancing every week. She is here to tell the class about her experiences of migrating to Australia. She was born the daughter of an English accountant in Egypt, a real lady back then, who had to come to Australia with her husband when Nasser gained power. She'd had maids in Egypt, but then she got to Australia found she had to do all her own washing and all her own ironing! And, oh! She cried and cried! She and Justine laugh together, perhaps imagining as I was this poor privileged girl weeping at her ironing board, and Justine replies with a similar story about her friend from India.
>
> At the end the children are invited to talk to the old woman. They gather around, clamouring to tell her about their own families' migrations, how they've been on planes themselves, and about their grandmas and grandpas. Few seem interested in asking questions of her, just three girls who look through the photo album of life back in Egypt. They giggle, 'Was that you? Your hair is funny'.
>
> Justine and I go to morning tea together. Justine tells me how pleased she is that the lesson went so well. But, I'm thinking, No, that's wrong! The kids were rude. They talked about themselves and didn't empathise. I don't know how to reply to Justine (Government School, author field notes, 29 May 2007).

This lesson does not seem to work as empathy to me. It does not seem to achieve any degree of 'seeing into' what it would have been to be this old woman in her past, nor what it is like to be her now. But, I want to suggest, this does not mean that no perspective-taking is achieved. It is just of a different type: a seeing with. Whatever Justine's intention was when she began the lesson, she is happy to guide the lesson in the direction she found it moving; and is wise enough to be pleased with the result.

Imagination as 'seeing with' is a notion that has more in common with Bakhtin's notion of the dialogic imagination than with the 'seeing into' of empathy. His work suggests that language and meaning are not fixed and speakers are not closed, message-sending bodies. Rather, at each moment the speaker makes a choice 'out of all the possible existing languages available to it at that moment' and speaks to 'transcribe its intention in this specific exchange' (Holquist 1981: xx). Thus, for him perspective-taking is ideally a partial and ongoing building of intersubjectivity rather than the wholesale move from self into other, from my shoes to yours. Our words open us, somewhat, to others and only for now.

Verran argues towards a similar ideal with her notion of 'postcolonial moments' which

> are made where disparate knowledge traditions abut and abrade, enmeshed, indeed often stuck fast, in power relations characteristic of colonizing. [...] [it] is not about retrieving a lost purity by overthrowing and uprooting an alien knowledge tradition. Rather, it might effect an opening up and loosening. Increasing possibilities for cooperation while respecting difference [...] Elaborating a postcolonial moment involves both making separations, and connecting by identifying sameness. [...] sameness in a postcolonial moment enables difference to be collectively enacted (Verran 2002: 730).

Let me put this simply. Different people live in the world differently, and sometimes they meet. The hope should not be for one or another way of living in the world to 'win', but to find ways to work together these ways of living. Doing so requires keeping the difference between the ways of living in sight, while also finding points of similarity. The result is new hybrid ways of living in the world, tiny or large, which work in the here and now.

How do Bahktin and Verran help us read the moment when children meet the old woman as a moment of 'seeing with'? In two ways. The first is that after the woman has finished her talk, this moment becomes a time of dialogue. What children try to do, in telling her about being on a plane and their grandparents, is to find points of common ground between them. These points are broad and simple, but they do identify sameness in their experiences. Now the children and the woman have found points at which their knowledge seems to provide sameness. From these points they could have perhaps found other similarities: they now could see that it was possible to have something in common with this woman so much older than they were. These are moments of intersubjectivity.

Second, some difference is brought to the centre of some children's attention. What I read as rude (the girls laughing over a photo of an old-fashioned hairstyle) might instead seem to be a moment of loosening, a point at which a gap is opened between these children's present and that woman's past. This is a moment at which children don't understand. Hairstyles in old photos have not been reduced to the explanation 'that was the fashion at that time'. Instead, as the children laugh at what seems to them to be a simply silly hairstyle, they see a point of difference between themselves and those photographed people. Recognising difference is vital if we are not to reduce all others' experiences to versions of what we ourselves have experienced already.

This then can be seen as an episode when perspectives are mutually changed by dialogue with another, albeit in minor ways and for only some children. These changes are not only those that pretend likeness. Children learn simultaneously that this old woman is the same as them in certain respects and also that she is unlike them: differences between growing up then (with that hair style), and growing up now (with these hairstyles), are enhanced by a refusal to reduce this difference to easy explanations like 'fashion'. This is perhaps what Justine recognised as successful, but what I had to question my own bodily expectations to see. By keeping difference in place, 'seeing with' can enable moving beyond the self as the index of knowledge. This however, is not the end of ways we can understand the routines of perspective-taking at this school, for it is not the only way the routines of listening and asking can play out.

## 'Seeing for': Different Futures

Justine lost her husband several years ago to cancer. She tells me of the revelation she had then – that imagination is vital for dealing with change and loss.

> At that time I needed to be able to imagine that I could be able to move on from that. That, that, yes I'm in a really bad spot, but that I could imagine that at some point, in a week or a couple of weeks I could imagine myself being two years down the path and being able to look back and say that I had made progress. And I guess sort of rethinking dreams of a future. So I think that and an ability to put myself in other people's situations and imagine, you know, their situations in life. So yeah, I think that I have come to understand the role of imagination is about being able to see endless possibilities and providing myself and others with different thinking of the possibilities and imagining, and understanding that if you can imagine yourself doing something you've got a greater chance of actually achieving it (Government School, author interview with teacher, 29 May 2007).

Justine is talking about the importance of imagination for coping and resilience. Having achieved this imagination in her own life, she realised that she had been unprepared by her own childhood: 'I came to understand how [a lack of imagination] had limited me, that I had never been able to imagine my life as being any different' (Government School, author interview with teacher, 29 May 2007). Now what she tells is of the importance of all these forms of perspective-taking – imagining oneself other – to embed in her class the ability to change. She is talking about an imagination that enables us to believe in the possibility of changing our lives in the face of crisis.

Vital to achieving this is the ability, as Justine puts it above, 'to put myself in other people's situations'. But this perspective-taking is not aimed towards empathy, towards knowing how another feels. Rather, it is aimed at seeing that there are wider possibilities for one's own life. By this mode, the children are to become capable of coping with personal and collective crises. This is achieved by giving an imaginary scenario that can be set against a current situation to give it scale and possibility. Perspective-taking now is not to 'know just how you feel' but to believe that things in one's own life could be different.

> A boy comes into Justine's classroom upset. She finds out what is wrong by asking him if he can explain to her while the class listens. He does and she asks some questions. The story emerges that his brother has broken his PlayStation. Justine agrees that it is right for him to be sad, saying that sometimes things happen that make us so sad we cannot even talk about them. But, she suggests, if he puts it on a continuum of the worst things that could have happened this morning, maybe he'll find that it's not so bad. Your brother could have been hurt, she puts as an example. Then she adds, 'He's probably upset about it too. What could you do to make your play together better?' (Government School, author field notes, 21 May 2007).

Here Justine gives the boy three options. He can focus on the moment of sadness, leaving it distinct and unnameable. Or he can mentally line it up in a string of worse possibilities, and by comparison find a perspective to give it scale. And finally, he can find ways to play better with his brother: PlayStations will remain intact, feelings will be spared, brothers will bond. The boy nods, sniffs, and sits down on the mat. The morning continues.

## CONCLUSION

'Seeing into', 'seeing with' and 'seeing for': these are the possibilities I have given to interpret the routines of perspective-taking that Justine and her colleagues work to embed in their students. At first I assumed that all perspective-taking was aimed at empathy – seeing how another feels. By taking account of the broader practices of this classroom as a corporeal, modest witness, I see now that things were more complex.

When a good teacher begins a lesson, they understand that the outcome cannot be predicted entirely. They can have goals, but learning, especially in a classroom of more than twenty children, is an unpredictable business. We saw Justine express pleasure and satisfaction over the outcomes of several of these lessons, and had I the presence of mind to ask, would likely have heard her give it for the others too. To me this suggests that she was not confused over what resulted, but that any or all of these types of perspective-taking met her hopes. She had broad intentions that could cope with some mangling.

I was unable to recognise this until I myself had done some imagination as perspective-taking. This required two steps. First, I had to recognise where I was seeing from and how this could be extended. I had to be honest about what I had hoped to see in this classroom, and acknowledge that there was more than one way to read events. I tried to become a more modest witness. Second, I had to try to recognise difference in the ways Justine and I were assessing lessons. Instead of thinking she was wrong, I had to think with her, achieving enough intersubjectivity to see her intentions as broader and richer than I had initially assumed.

My argument here, then, is that participant-observation researchers always face the challenge of contemplating where they 'see from'. When working with others, it is often necessary to wonder about their perspectives and intentions, and, because of the resistances they face in practice, these will be subject to ongoing mangling. Researchers should always work to imagine other ways to see more modestly – to see into and from, to see with, and for.

**7**

# HAVING A FRIEND

*A Special Classroom and the Making of Relationships*

Boys from the local high school are here over recess. Part of their community work this year is to teach games and hobbies to the kids. It hasn't been working, according to Amanda, a grade three teacher. The high school boys don't know how to get the kids to share equipment or follow the rules of games. The kids are confused and excited, and some, says Amanda, start acting all macho male to assert that they're not 'special'. Just then, a boy grabs the tube of black paint from the desk set up for painting and runs across the dry, sunny field to the posts that hold up the shade cloth. His hands are smeared in paint, and he rubs it all over the post until Amanda runs over to stop him. 'What beautiful finger painting,' she says, 'but that's enough now'. In her grasp and with her words, he calms down and allows himself to be led to the outside sink. Together they wash his hands. 'This is how we wash our hands, wash our hands, wash our hands', Amanda sings softly.

Two boys, hand in hand, run past where I stand. One suddenly sits. The other tries to pull him up. 'I didn't say sit down', he says, sounding frustrated. 'I said, "let's run over there and find the treasure."' The seated boy lets himself be pulled up. They run on.

Amanda comes back towards me saying that the boy who took the paint has got out of the play area. She is on duty and has to stay here, so she asks me to have a look for him behind the school. But, she warns, if I see him I should find someone else to deal with him. He'd be too strong for me. I unhook the orange plastic that acts as a gate, and walk a few steps. I see the boy, huge though young, all in black, lumbering surprisingly quickly towards me. A teacher is already in pursuit. I watch as she tries to hold onto him, and as four more teachers rush to help. Together they succeed, as he grunts and hits out, to steer him towards the small fenced enclosure at the side of the playground. He is locked in for the rest of recess (Special School, author field notes, 9 October 2007).

IN THIS STORY OF A RECESS AT A SCHOOL FOR LOW-IQ STUDENTS, WE SEE many people working hard to make collective life work: the boys from the high school, the teacher Amanda, and the boy trying to play a game of pretence. We also see this work breaking down, and more work done to try to recover forms of cooperation. This work is variously attempted with equipment like paint and sports gear; words that pretend the scenarios of finger painting and treasure hunting; and bodies grasping and leading. These are all moments, some playful and some forceful, to achieve the co-construction of goals. Underlying all this is imagination.

Imagination is used, I will argue here, to create a belief that disparate people have shared goals. Moreover, imagination is necessary to form the bonds between people necessary for the achievement of those goals. What I hope to argue, in short, is that the concept of and the relationships necessary to cooperative group life are achieved through particular routines for doing imagination.

Participation and observation at a school for low-IQ children made these processes of material, coordinated group action obvious. Because these children were poor at working together, or even recognising the need to work together, the methods that teachers used to teach cooperation were particularly clear. Above we have seen the consequences for various people – teachers and children alike – when the imaginative routines they have attempted go wrong. Posts get painted, games are abruptly stopped, children are chased and enclosed. But we will find that the same types of imaginative routines are worked at other schools also.

What I tell in this chapter is animated by a great admiration for the teachers whose classrooms I participated in. As I felt overwhelmed by the onward rush of events, I saw teachers coping with ease. Used to having time to reflect, I didn't know how to deal with the ever-changing needs of children, but these teachers made it seem simple. In this chapter, I try to do justice to these talented teachers, telling stories of events rushing on and teachers responding. Theirs is a particular imaginative skill, and one that has nothing to do with representation. They are seasoned interveners, and the passages they walk are hugely unpredictable. They use their own imaginations and that of their students to solve a distinct public problem that has to do with making 'the other' socially capable.

What is performed at Special School, I will suggest, are imaginative practices aiming to get children to relate to materials and other people by providing a structure in which this relating makes sense. We see this most clearly in the moments of play that fail. The two boys are playing a game of pretence that bumps its way along with the guidance of the more powerful player. He reminds the other player of the purpose of running across the field and he says again that this is a joint goal – let's go find the treasure. Running across the field together again makes sense, and the sitting boy rises and continues. The students from the high school meanwhile fail because they can't get the children to understand the shared system (rules) needed for their games to work. The children do not seem to understand that for the game to work they must follow specific conventions and that they have to act together to enact these. They do not have an imaginative scenario that will make sense of the game to be played. In one game, the shared goal and rules made sense because it was embedded in an imaginative story; in the other game, there was no imaginative story and no success. Recognising this suggests that play is important for our learning to relate to others and to materials within some overarching real or imaginary system. Play, in this view, is a way of learning to act together in communities of practice.[*]

What is also special about the imaginative routines of this school is the skill of the teachers. Imagination enables these teachers to flexibly relate themselves to unpredictable child needs via people, materials, words, and structures. It can never be taken for granted that children already agree that they are part of

---

[*] There is huge debate about what play is 'for', if anything. Perhaps my favourite answer is that provided by Brian Sutton-Smith, who suggests that, given the great variety of play types and practices, play is 'for' learning adaptive variability (Sutton-Smith 1997). For other impressive accounts of how play has been dealt with in scholarship, see Schwartzman (1978); Goldman (1998).

a group with some shared goal. Nor can it be assumed that they understand or are committed to following any system of rules. These things are forgotten or ignored, and children are locked behind fences. Thus, Amanda does not refer to particular elements in a system of rules. She cannot assume that this boy knows that he is not allowed to put paint all over the posts because he knows he must care for school property, though this is one of the school rules. Instead she tells of beautiful and complete finger painting, claiming to value his actions but see them as no longer necessary. Next we see him running away, breaking the rules of being a good knower (fitting in with collective systems of behaviour) or having good knowledge (that, for example, due to the systems of rules and discipline, he will be caught and punished for leaving). He is large, angry, and unpredictable. Therefore, teachers must rush to seize and enclose him where his actions will remain uncertain, but will now be constrained. Without the power of already shared systems to govern behaviour, teachers must find ways, every time, to guide children towards better behaviours for their learning and cooperating. This takes a certain imagination, one that is flexible and responsive. These teachers, then, display impressive talents at responding to sudden particulars in ways that will keep group life as together as possible.

Learning happens in relationships with other people and things – what is important about the imagination at Special School is its role in making these relationships. I will make this argument with scholars who suggest that successful learning is achieved by membership in communities of practice. I then return to this particular case and ask why this imagination is so obvious at Special School: what is special about Special School? We then look at how imaginative routines done at other schools make children relate in different ways. And we will close with an account of what makes the teachers who work at Special School so impressive, a close that returns us to the teachers' relational imagination.

## THINKING WITH SCHOLARS ABOUT THINKING WITH OTHERS

The scholars I appeal to here suggest that the common picture of learning as adding to the store of information in a mind is incomplete. What is revealed instead is learners acting with material in ways that are deemed wrong (and corrected) or correct (and extended) by those around them. It is when we know *how to do things* – such as how to categorise information or objects, or to use the right words to refer, or the order of steps to solve a number problem – that we can be said to have learnt. Lucy Suchman (1987), for example, argues that the cognitive models that were used to build artificial intelligence failed because they exactly ignored such socially and materially situated aspects of human thinking. To be an intelligent agent in this new picture would mean noticing and gradually adapting to others' ways of talking and acting with each other and with the materials around them. This is the case for the most seemingly objective forms of knowing, such as mathematics. Jean Lave, for example, shows that 'everyday' mathematical ability is a matter of adopting various techniques for using the materials available rather than working through singular processes of mental computation (Lave 1988). Learning mathematics, in other words, would not only mean access to a mental storehouse of information. Instead, it would mean knowing how to use mental and physical objects in ways that achieve the goal sought. These are not lone mental activities, but require being embedded in the social and material systems that mathematics is to achieve: calculating a supermarket bill, or weaving a carpet.

Talking about learning in this way shifts the site of knowing away from lone agents. Attention is instead paid to the collectivity necessary to, and produced by, the course of acting together. This was evident to Edwin Hutchins as he wondered how naval ships could be sailed successfully even though no one person had all the knowledge necessary to manipulate the mechanics of the ship or direct its navigation. His answer was that the 'boundaries of the cognitive unit of analysis [should be moved] out beyond the skin of the individual person' (Hutchins 1995: xiv). His book looks therefore at the complex of words and gestures that kept this group knowledge coordinated well enough that the ship could be brought into port.

This way of talking about learning also shifts what knowledge objects are. Perhaps, as Verran suggests, objects of knowledge, like numbers, are also produced in moments of acting with other people and with materials. Verran suggests that numbers are produced in our interactions with numbered objects. To understand her argument, we need the concept of interpellation developed by

Louis Althusser. Interpellation for Althusser means to find oneself part of the relations of power as soon as action is taken to pull you in. A policeman calls 'hey you', and you, in turning, become subject to him, subject to the material and ideological structures of the state (Althusser 1977: 160–165). Similarly, according to Verran, the writing or saying of a numeral in relation to a material thing calls us to recognise it as a number, a sign of material order or quantity. Her story runs like this:

> As I stand before a rickety market stall with tomatoes arranged into a small pile, exuding their tomato smell in the hot sun, "ogún" sounds as a pile of five small tomatoes is pointed to. The pointing-at-tomato-pile-while-at-a-stall-in-a-market interpellates, hails, the numeral *ogún* as numbered-tomato-pile (Verran, 2001: 102).

'Ogún' is made sensible by the sounding of the word, simultaneous to the pointing at five tomatoes.

In making these various arguments about the collective enacting of knowledge, these scholars reiterate and extend Ian Hacking's suggestion that we talk about knowing not as representing, but as intervening. To Hacking the real is not something static that we represent, but something that we come to know through our interactions with it (Hacking 1983: 146).

All these theorists take for granted that collective routines are easy, or easy enough, for us naturally social humans. This is not always the case: children in particular must learn the necessity of, and the skills required for, thinking together with others and with materials. How do we learn to become successfully related to others in our goals, our bodily routines and our thinking? These questions are particularly pertinent at Special School, where teachers describe their children as concrete and egotistical.

## Friendship and Thinking with Others

> I'd really like them to have a friend. That's basically [...] when they leave here a lot of our kids don't really have friends, and that's, that connection

just doesn't happen for them, and we do a lot of stuff on empathy and a lot of stuff on how to speak to people and being a good friend and that. Their social group is a lot smaller than other people's, and they often don't get the skills, those sort of innate skills that other people seem to just develop. And in this [class]room there's a couple of friendships, and that is just the best thing, and that they can just chat as friends, and that's quite rare in this setting. So yeah, I'd like them to have a friend (Special School, author interview with teacher, 26 October 2007).

These are words that Special School teacher Diane uses in an interview when asked what imaginative skills she would like her children to have when they leave her classroom. For her, children's friendships are difficult and precious accomplishments, based on a type of connection that 'just doesn't happen for them'. These skills and the ensuing connections are mysterious: 'innate skills that other people seem to just develop'. Diane takes these skills to be basic necessities for living happy lives. These are issues for the building of relationships, strong self-esteem, and personal resilience. On the other side, the lack of interpersonal skills has a cruel face that might lead these children into social and legal conflict. Diane explains that 'I worry about the lack of empathy with a couple. That's what I worry about, because I think that as they go through life they could end up more in trouble' (Special School, author interview with teacher, 26 October 2007).

Teachers at other schools agree that building good relationships is necessary for success in life, but their concern rests less with the social issues and more with the question of learning. Interpersonal bonds are central to Justine's understanding of the success of her children later in their lives. When I ask her whether she is worried that her children might not meet the increasingly formal, Australia-wide 'benchmarking' standards for literacy and numeracy, she says no. She explains that her children always do well in high school education because they have high-level interpersonal skills (Government School, author field notes, 25 May 2007). They will learn because they are good at relating.

## IDENTIFYING THE FIELD: A CLASS ON THE MARGINS

Let us move inside from the playground we opened this chapter with. Where are we? The classroom mainly referred to in this chapter is marginal in several senses. Located on the outskirts of Melbourne, in an area that has grown rapidly in recent years, it is quite literally a place on the margins. This has made it easy for authorities to ignore. The school has been built for a much smaller number of pupils than are now enrolled, and after years of waiting extensive additions are finally being built to ease some of the problems of overcrowding.

Our classroom here is part of what is designated a 'special' school. With this appellation, the school is made different from what are referred to by these and other teachers as 'mainstream' schools. The children likewise take on this identity; they are special children, set apart from 'mainstream' children. It is both their intelligence and their behaviour that leads them to be defined this way.

Most of the children here are boys – in the class I work in, it is six out of eight. Teachers tell me that this is because the weight of disorders associated with low IQ like autism and ADHD is carried more heavily in male genetics. It is also suggested that boys are more likely to be disruptive to a mainstream class and therefore more likely to be classified as suitable in IQ terms for this school. A low-IQ girl in a mainstream school is more likely to be ignored. It is marginal, 'anti-social behaviour', not just intelligence, that defines a child as 'special'.

Once at this school children are further defined by intelligence, with the school body broken into groups by a combination of age and level of functioning. The class I spend time with are 'high functioning' grade fours, and according to their teachers, are remarkably able for this school. So by membership in this class, children are set above most of the children at the school. But ironically this leads them to even more awareness that they are 'special'. In the class I work in, three children attend a 'mainstream' school for a number of days each week, ranging from one day a week to four. Another child was removed from his mainstream school because of his behavioural problems. At this school they are relatively normal, the smart kids. At their other primary schools they are likely even more obviously 'special' – the kids who are there only sometimes, the dumb kids.

Each classroom is managed by two adults, one a trained teacher and the other a trained integration aide. Most of the staff are female, and many explain that they have taken work here because it is better suited to motherhood than work at a mainstream school. This teaching, though physically and psychologically exhausting, needs little preparation or planning. It is regarded by staff as easier and less time-consuming work than teaching in a 'mainstream' school.

The teachers are paid more than integration aides. If a teacher is away, a relief teacher must be put in their place. In theory an integration aide, regardless of skill or experience, cannot be given full responsibility for a class. In practice, however, an integration aide such as Michaela in the classroom I spent my time in, might do large amounts of sole teaching, both in specialist subjects like computing, and when Diane, the teacher, was away and the relief teacher was not sure how to proceed. This work is not formally recognised, nor even officially allowed. Until an integration aide gets formal teaching qualifications she will be taken as 'assistant' regardless of the work she does. Part of my hope here is to highlight the skill of both the women in this classroom, the talented 'special' school teachers, marginal to the mainstream education system, and the integration aides, marginal to the proper work of the 'special' classroom.

Finally, as I've suggested above, this classroom is marginal to the systems of sociality and knowledge that direct life and learning in other schools I visited. The levels of accomplishment and potential that children show necessitate different and lower goals. Some grade four children are being taught to brush their teeth regularly, others to listen while someone is speaking, still others to stay in their own classroom. The children in our high-functioning classroom are learning to take responsibility for a classroom job (sweeping the back room, putting up the chairs) and to read, write, and count.

Here, with children impaired in their ability to understand what are taken to be basic concepts elsewhere, a question is raised. What should be taught and to what end? The school aim is defined in the parents' booklet, which states that children should learn to live as independently as possible in the community. But how can these children be taught to integrate into the community? The answer I will put forward here, describing the work of teachers at Special School and elsewhere, sees teachers responding to opportunities to build skills in social bonding and group thinking, and helping children to understand themselves as related to the structures and systems they live within. Imagination at this school is used to produce children as knowers able to relate themselves to society.

## THE MINEFIELD OF DISTRIBUTED COGNITION

'Bang', the physical education (PE) teacher calls out. 'Bang' repeats Dwyane, and rushes around the side to try the course again. Today they're supposed to be working on their teamwork by collectively trying to work out the right way to step through a four-by-four grid of hoops laid on the ground. It is a minefield, their teacher has told them. He alone can see the way through because, he tells them as he pulls his sunglasses on, he has magic glasses. All he'll say is 'bang' to tell them when they've stepped in the wrong hoop. The children have to work out the correct way through the minefield by watching each other and talking about it. They rush through, without stopping to talk or think or take proper turns. 'Bang', says the teacher, 'bang, bang'.

Eventually one boy works it out, and another copies him. The teacher points it out, 'see, Victor's done it. Watch what he's done'. They keep jumping from hoop to hoop, while their teacher says 'Bang. Bang. If you've worked it out, go tell your friends'. Finally five get across the hoops in a row, and now start to call out the colours so their classmates can get across. Otherwise they'll all have to start again. Logan is excited, yelling 'we did it' and 'it went bang, bang, bang, bang, bang, bang' (Special School, author field notes, 25 October 2007).

This lesson has been designed to make this class better at working in a group. PE teacher John tells the class that the task is hard because they need to get eight people thinking as if they are one person. He is teaching children the need for attention and communication to achieve shared aims. Only if they watch and talk to each other will they all manage to make it through the minefield in one go.

Imagination is used here to create a scenario that requires children to work together within a system – the hoops are a minefield they must cross together, pretends John. He works this imaginative scenario throughout the game by looking through his 'magic glasses' and calling 'bang' when the children step in the 'wrong' hoop.

For a lesson of this kind to succeed the imaginary scenario must embed both the goal and the process by which it is possible to achieve it. The children must be aware of the overall aim – to get the class across the minefield – and the way they can do this – by taking turns to attempt to cross. By choosing a good scenario, John has embedded rules and processes neatly within the task. But the higher aim of the lesson is for children to think of themselves as a group, and enjoy the bonds they are forming. These are complex bonds of trust, authority, support, and assistance. Again it is the scenario itself that makes these bonds happen – the children have to teach and learn from each other in order to get through the minefield. They find this exciting: 'bang bang bang bang bang'. It is because they enjoy the scenario that they will allow the teacher to hold authority. This can be visualised as forming a circular logic. John must make students trust his authority; they must authorise him to make the rules (Benjaminsen 2007).

The lesson's success here has rested on three conditions all achieved through John's use of an imaginary scenario that has laid the system and goal down clearly. These conditions are that the children know how to go about achieving the shared goal; that they are enfolded into and communicate as a group; and that they enjoy being so enfolded. These three conditions are necessary for imaginative scenarios to clot children as cognitive groups. This happens in other ways at other schools.

## IMAGINATION AND SHARED WORK
### Imagination for Group Building

At two schools I witness the purposeful use of imaginary games intended to help children from non-English speaking backgrounds become better able to engage with the linguistic conventions of their school community. Imaginative play, in both these cases, is to be the process by which children will become more adept at handling the words, sentences, and interpersonal relationships seen as vital to their membership of an English-speaking school. Through imaginative play, they will become members of the larger linguistic group.

In one case, that of Government School, imaginative play is encouraged by the supply of various types of play materials. In one area of a large hall are dressing-up clothes arranged in a 'house'; in another, plastic facsimiles of money and foods; in yet another are large foam mats and tubes. Children are taken out of their classrooms to play with children from other classes with whatever they wish. They will then gather to tell the larger group what games they have played.

In the other case, that of Catholic School, it is the space itself that is to encourage imaginary games. In the account that circulates at the school, a teacher listening to her children play in their cubby (a small play space) noticed the complex language they were using as they enjoyed their game. She suggested a cubby be built at this school to provide a space for the many first-generation refugee and immigrant children whose numbers were rapidly increasing. In response, the school raised funds to build a 'village': a building in four linear sections, each open at the front. Staff call one room 'the house'; one has plants growing and is called the garden; one has a cross above the door and is called either the church or the hospital; and the final one has a counter around the front edge and is either a shop or a restaurant.

In both cases teachers assume that providing the material objects and/or settings for imaginative play will direct children naturally towards performing routines of imaginative play that will draw them together as groups. They will dress up, build, and otherwise enact imaginative scenarios they create together using their linguistic resources. The games they are most easily enabled to play are taken by the teachers to be those that mime likely future roles – shopping, having houses, gardens, and children, going to church, and hospital. This will serve the purpose of advancing their skills using the various objects of language – words, sentences, and so on. Certainly they will learn the clause 'let's pretend…' that Gregory Bateson, and those who have followed, have argued is a tool needed for marking and making shifts from 'real' to 'playful' designations of parts of the world (Bateson 1971; Stewart 1978).

## What Kind of Group Life?

It is easy to assume that children will want to be members of cooperative groups. Play is seen as a tool to enable the achievement of this desire. But this desire is not necessarily already real, but is something that is worked towards. Nor is it simply the case that groups will be founded on cooperation. I will suggest that the structure of games the teacher plays with the children is important. It matters because this spills into the bonds that children have with others and into their enjoyment of having these bonds. But what type of bonds should be built – those of pleasure, cooperation, or competition?

During PE and some other lessons, teachers introduce and cement notions of what a game is and what it is for. Are games essentially cooperative or competitive? Are they played for pleasure, or for victory, or for an individual's physical skills? The ways these questions are answered in teacher structured games bleed into the modes of game-playing children engage in during their free time. Hence, teacher structured games have some impact on the types of interpersonal relationships built 'freely' by children. Games have a big impact on how children are able to imagine themselves related to others.

We have already seen John purposefully choose a game for PE that will help develop notions of teamwork in his children. These, it is explicitly hoped, will spill into their classroom and playground lives to some extent. We see something similar at Steiner School where children in grade four play cooperatively at highly complex imaginary games, and PE involves first a warm-up then time for skill development. To warm up children are to play a 'fun' game, 'crocodile, crocodile', for example. This is a game of tag that pretends that the space of the tennis courts is a crocodile infested river. One child stands in the middle being 'crocodile'. The rest chant 'crocodile, crocodile, can I cross the river? If not, why not? What's your favourite colour?' The 'crocodile' responds by naming a colour, and all wearing clothes of that colour have to run through the 'river' and risk being caught by the 'crocodile'. If caught, they become 'crocodiles' too. The last child who is still 'safe' is the next lone crocodile. In this game oppositions are transitory; victory passes gradually to one child who wins only to stand against the rest of their class who are now formed as a team with shared interests (Steiner School, author field notes, 6 June 2007). Here children choose to participate in mixed gender, large group imaginary games during their morning and lunch breaks.

At the wealthy Independent School, games in PE are structured quite differently. Here skill development is built into simple, yet highly competitive games. A class favourite is 'war ball', usually played in gendered teams: boys vs girls. In this game, whoever has the ball has to throw it at a member of the other team who, if hit, is then 'out'. The winners are the team that gets all their opponents 'out' first. As the name suggests, this game is structured around the metaphor 'games are war'. Teams are fixed and, when based on biological sex, are inescapable. Individual success and team victory are achieved by the violence of a well-aimed throw at the body of another. The boys usually win, and if the teacher joins in it is always to support the girls. Most children clearly enjoy this game, asking to play it and participating with enthusiasm.

Interestingly, imaginative play is rare among children in the grade four age group at Independent School. Gender separations continue into free time. During lunchtimes most boys from this class play soccer. The girls in the class complain that there is little to do at lunchtime now that they are this age. They explain that they usually spend their time talking together. They say they used to play soccer, but the boys never gave them the ball. The structures of game-playing witnessed in PE seem to be in a feedback relationship to the free play of children. Boys play skill-based competitive games. Girls who try to join in, regardless of their skill, complain that no boy ever passes them the ball. Furthermore, play is designated as competitive by its very nature. Imaginative games are 'babyish' (Independent School, writing piece, 16 April 2007: 1,7). One boy in the class is not welcomed in this game system – he spends lunchtimes alone in the library or idly outside. Options to play games that are not sport have been cut: when I ask him what games he plays that are not sport he does not understand the question – in asking 'what do you mean?' he seems to say there are no games that are not sport. Girls suffer this same break; they do not play, they talk. Boys are able to build social relationships of competition based upon bodily skill in games. Refused access to competitive games, girls build social relationships in cooperative talk. Unlike Steiner children, none of them are building social relationships by playing imaginative games.

In my reading of these teacher-structured and child-chosen games, we see some children being explicitly encouraged to see themselves as linked by cooperative game-playing. Other children learn to engage in competitive forms of play across gendered lines, and this limits their engagement in imaginative and cooperative game-playing during free time. These forms of game-playing are structured by teachers' use of metaphors – rivers to cross, wars to fight. It matters how games are imagined. In games, certain modes of pleasurable relating to others are legitimated. Others are marginalised. In games, the types of bonds children are to have and enjoy are founded.

Of course, cooperation is not taught only by game-playing – children can work together in all manner of projects. But important too are the modes of group-making that are enacted within the classroom itself. These depend on certain modes of teaching that I designate as relational. These we will examine now, thinking particularly about the implications of class-making for the possibilities of learning.

## THE RELATIONAL TEACHER

If collective knowing is achieved when members of a group build material and semiotic systems to share their thinking, what is the role of the teacher? I believe it is as a member of *and* authority over classes. This is achieved materially though classroom layout, in the performance of authority known as interpellation, and in the imaginative bonds developed through work on shared tasks.

Membership in class groups is normally achieved through a mixture of familiar material and semiotic techniques. Teachers call the group a collective noun like 'class', 'children', 'grade four', or 'room three'. In such forms of naming, the individuals are gathered as members of that group. The group is seated in desks arranged in particular shapes that produce certain relations with each other and with the teacher. Desks arranged in rows force the class to observe together the teacher as authority. This happens at Steiner School. Desks arranged in a semicircle around the mat and board that places the teacher as authority and simultaneously creates a middle space for shared dialogue that includes the teacher, as at Catholic School. Desks arranged in clumps form the class as constituted by smaller groups, and the teacher moving between functions as authority over all. We see this at Independent School, Government School, and Special School.

It is in the very moment of a teacher calling the 'class' to collectively act that the children cease to be simply individuals and become also a group subject to the teacher. In making the class a group, the teacher makes her authority. This is an example of 'interpellation'. In Althusser's story, a policeman hails a man. 'Hey you' the policeman calls, and the man turns. In the moment of that turn the man is made subject to the policeman's authority, and in being so, the man becomes also subject to the state formation that gives the policeman power (Butler 1995; Althusser 1977; Law 2000; Verran 2001). In a similar way, it is in the moment of calling by saying 'class, come sit on the mat' that the teacher interpellates the class as a group all subordinated to her authority.

Discipline can be exercised by appealing to these group relations, for example, by reminding children of the responsibilities entailed in membership of the group. Teachers may say to a disruptive child, 'The class are all waiting for you'. Discipline can be undermined when a child ceases to feel part of the group, as when a disruptive child is singled out repeatedly or sent out of the room. At these moments, the power afforded to the teacher by her material and semiotic acts of group-making are evident.

I suggest that the good teacher in a classroom is not just an authority, but also a member of the group and its processes. This is a matter of choosing material and semiotic acts that require her to be active within the class fabric. This requires her to listen to and act with her children, to their words and ways of using material. She has more authority, but this should be understood as meaning that she has more knowledge about how to use words and materials, and that she is trusted with more rights to draw out some ideas and squash others. Authority in this interpretation of learning and teaching is that more faces will look at her when she speaks. Throughout the year they will continue to look as she shows, again and again, her mastery over the material and linguistic tools suitable for their age and interesting to them as individuals. These will include the material and linguistic tools of discipline.

Good teaching to achieve the collective enactment of knowing requires one to be part of the collectivity being built. It is a matter of being an active, responsive, and responsible member of the group of people and objects. It is not simply a matter of telling people what to do.

What does this look like? Here is one example.

When we get to the music room the music teacher is not there. She is away, and through administrative blunder has not been replaced for the day. Michaela, though 'only' an integration aide, runs the lesson while the real teacher (a relief today) sits plucking at his guitar. Roderick asks if they can sing 'our names' as a warm-up and Michaela agrees. She starts picking up chairs and putting them in a row. The children help and she moves to find the right CD. She calls each child in turn to stand up the front facing the class. Together we sing with the voices on CD, until they sing 'please sing me your name'. Alone now, the child at the front sings 'My name is _____', and we all join in again. 'You have to: this is a concert. Your audience are waiting', Michaela tells Victor when he tries to refuse his turn. Michaela and I take our turns at the front.

Next, seeing Dwyane clapping his hands on his knees, Michaela says 'I think we're in the rhythm mood. Let's do some percussion'. She begins collecting the drums, scrapers, and triangles from around the room and piling them on the desk. 'What else do we need?' she asks the children, and asks, as she finds instruments, 'What's this called?' She does not know which CD contains the song they used last week for percussion, so she says 'We'll improvise'. The kids have fun hitting their drums and scraping their scrapers in time with the song; Cindy even starts dancing in time.

Watching this succeed, Michaela decides on more percussion, getting out the set of drums of various sizes. We all sit on the floor in a circle, each with a drum. Michaela tells the class that each drum is a village and they're used for talking to each other. Hitting them hard, as Dwyane has been, might be a way to say that you're starting a war. Michaela selects pairs to 'talk' to each other on their drums. Each hits a rhythm, listens, and replies. Michaela asks them what they were saying in words – 'we were starting a war'; 'we were saying nice things, like "I like that you're my friend"'. Michaela and I have a turn, and she asks the children 'What do you think we were talking about?' 'You were whispering,' comes the reply, 'you were gossiping'. Lesson over, we walk back to the classroom. I praise Michaela, and she says that since they seemed into it, why not keep it going? (Special School, author field notes, 19 October and 26 October 2007).

I have told this lesson in full because I believe it shows Michaela performing a style of teaching that is seldom recognised as skilful. It might seem that Michaela is just allowing whatever happens to happen, but in fact, in responding to and expanding on what the children are enjoying, she is advancing the children's collective knowing lives in two ways. First, she takes the opportunity to teach the material handling of objects: voices in musical time, percussion instruments. Second, by calling the singing 'a concert' and the drumbeats 'villages in conversation', Michaela forms the classes into these groups: concert performers, and community of villages. Using this imaginary scenario, she enhances the class's sense of their group identity and uses this identity to make group knowledge. She teaches rhythm and volume, turn-taking and friendship. This she does without planning, responding creatively to the needs and desires of the children, and to the possibilities embedded in the objects around them. This is what I call imaginative relational teaching: to take what is happening now and imaginatively move it forward in ways that are positive for her children.

## CONCLUSION

In this chapter I have argued that much of what teachers use imagination for is to help children to think and work together. This, I have suggested, is particularly obvious at Special School, and for two reasons. First, because children are deemed not imaginative, with the bulk of concern centring on the problems this may cause for future relationships. Diane hopes simply that her children will have a friend, or at least will be able to avoid the interpersonal misunderstandings that lead to social and legal trouble. Important for teaching this imagination to children were imaginative scenarios that made sense of bodily processes and rules, including for language use, and that let children see themselves as members of groups with certain types of relationship.

Secondly, teachers at Special School take as an intrinsic part of their own practice the imagination that helps them to work and think with children moment by moment. I have called this 'relational teaching' and have said it is achieved when a teacher is flexible to changing situations and is responsive to children's changing needs and interests.

I relate this to what scholars like Suchman, Lave, and Hutchins have argued about the importance of collectivities in many types of human thinking and acting. Discussing the disparate topics of artificial intelligence, mathematics learning, and naval ship sailing, they share the conviction that knowing is a matter of knowing how to interact with materials and other people in socially conventional ways.

# DOING THE RELATIONAL

*Imagining Connections and Separations*

In today's literacy lesson, the text is a song. Children are sitting on the mat while Mrs Rich operates the CD player. She starts the song, but it's the wrong one. Children giggle, looking at each other and miming dance moves. Mrs Rich, suppressing a smile, lets it play right through. She finds the song she had intended. It is called 'My Place'. It is in country style, with lyrics about a home in a small Australian country town. Mrs Rich lets it play once, then she asks the class to list some 'graphic organisers'. Children suggest various ways of arranging information – Venn diagrams, webs, mind maps – and Mrs Rich writes them on the board. From the list she selects the Y-chart. She draws a large Y shape on the board, writing 'looks like', 'sounds like', and 'feels like', one each in a segment. She explains: she will play the song several more times, and each subsequent time they will be thinking 'what does it look like?', then 'what does it sound like?', and finally, 'what does it feel like?' She says that just like good readers, 'good listeners make connections'. She repeats, slowly, 'good listeners make connections'.

She plays the song three more times, and after each playing asks the children to share with their partners and then with the class the connections they made. First, they are to give connections that describe what they saw while they listened, then what they heard, and, after the final playing, what they felt.

The children share their mental connections, what the song made them imagine. The assortment includes that it looked dusty; that there are not many houses around; that it is a little house with a gate to the back yard; that there were sounds of birds; a guitar playing; water boiling on a barbecue; and that it sounds like twenty years ago. Connections made to feelings are the most interesting. Children say, 'it made me feel great'; 'it's cold there'; 'it's sad because his friends only visit sometimes'; 'sad because my cousins live in the country and I don't often get to see them'; 'I felt bad because people were teasing him'; 'sad because it made me think of my old house'. Mrs Rich says she is surprised. She had thought it was a happy song (Catholic School, author field notes, 31 August 2007).

IMAGINATION, IN MRS RICH'S WORDS AND IN HER PRACTICE, IS 'A THINKING tool' (Catholic School, author interview with teacher, 11 September 2007). More specifically, it is a tool for making connections. These connections might be between the lyrics of a song and the feelings, sights, and sounds they evoke. They may be between one book and another, or between an idea and its personal meaning. Mrs Rich uses this imagination extensively in her literacy classes, often asking children to link the stories they hear to other stories or other experiences they have had. The repertoire she calls on, and which is familiar to her class, are 'text to text', 'text to self', and 'text to world' connections (Catholic School, author field notes, 30 August 2007). The routine here is to first tell a partner what connections one has thought of, and, if chosen by the teacher, to share with the class. This is summed up in Mrs Rich's oft repeated instruction 'think, pair, share'. In her class, then, imagination is the set of routines whereby the teacher requests and students offer (usually verbally) connections that link the here and now to some mental other. Each time they make connections they are also making separations, for example distinguishing hearing, seeing, and feeling as ways to experience the song. What they do each time is make synthetic – and potentially new – thoughts.

This is how Mrs Rich uses imagination to solve public problems – to form habits of rich connective thinking in her students. All teachers, in fact, use imagination to help children make connections. As we shall see throughout this concluding chapter, however, their ways of making connections and the patterns of thought they encourage children towards vary greatly.

In this conclusion, I apply the lesson I learnt in Mrs Rich's class that imagination can be performed by making mental connections and separations explicit. To this end, I will work to make explicit the patterns of thinking encouraged in each classroom. I will argue that some teachers favour linear patterns of connection-making while others favour thinking as ways of making sets. I will suggest that each of these ways of thinking encouraged by teachers works to separate nature and culture in particular ways. A relational metaphysics suggests, though, that this is not how the world really is. Instead it is a complex web of nature and culture. Opening and closing this concluding chapter with Mrs Rich, I will suggest that only her way of using imagination to make connections properly engages with this web. In Mrs Rich we find a relational teacher, but one who does not stop at responsively and flexibly relating children and materials, but who makes surprising things relate conceptually. We find a teacher solving public problems by making complex connection-making habitual for her children.

## RICH THINKING

Mrs Rich calls on children to use imagination to make connections throughout the curriculum and the school day. Doing so, she is making imagination into the type of thinking tool demanded by a new curriculum, the Victorian Essential Learning Standards (VELS). 'Thinking Processes' is a new part of the curriculum these teachers are working with, intended to be interdisciplinary. Since it is not meant to fit in one subject only, it is hoped that teachers will return their students to 'thinking' throughout the school day. To do this they are asked to 'model skilful and effective thinking and make their own thinking explicit as part of their everyday practice' (Victorian Curriculum and Assessment Authority, 2006).

But how to model thinking, and exactly what types of connections to emphasise, is up to each teacher. As Mrs Rich says, 'Where does it tell you how to deliver anything? And I don't think it really tells us. So it's totally up to you' (Catholic School, author interview with teacher, 11 September 2007). As we will see, each teacher I worked with modelled different patterns of connection-making, and thereby directed children towards different forms of thinking.

For Mrs Rich the key thinking tool is 'imagination as connection making'. It happens not only in literacy classes, but even in maths. There the focus is on making connections between numbers and then describing those connections. I see an example of this when Mrs Rich gets her class doing mental arithmetic. Writing a list of equations on the board, she asks children for the answers and for the strategies they used to get them. Children describe what they say to themselves in their minds; processes of rounding up and down, of estimating with the help of neater equations, and so on. Discouraging them from simply picturing the written equation in their heads, Mrs Rich praises the creative con-nections made so long as the correct answer is reached. Perhaps surprisingly, she certainly does consider this to be imagination. 'Maths problems, we have discussions about, that mental computation is extremely important, so what's the thinking going on in their mind? They need to verbalise it' (Catholic School, author interview with teacher, 11 September 2007).

There are several reasons this class practises such an imagination. In this school, a Catholic primary in a low-income area, there is a diversity of back-grounds and abilities. In Mrs Rich's class there are three Sudanese refugee chil-dren who know very little of the English language and who have little experience with the many tacit social and intellectual skills needed in an Australian school. There is a large group whose English is impeccable, but who do not speak English at home. Their initial thinking has been done in some other language system. And there are two children diagnosed with learning disabilities and assisted by an integration aide some of the time. For these various children, the otherwise hidden ways of thinking in the English language need to be made explicit. Moreover, it is a large class, and restless. As Mrs Rich tells me, she needs a large range of activities at the forefront of her mind so that she can keep order and enhance the enjoyment of learning. Her teaching technique must draw this diverse student body into one subject. Open-ended tasks and requests to draw personally pertinent connections are ways she does so. An obvious necessary condition for learning to be achieved in this classroom is this teacher: highly intelligent, very experienced, and blessed with huge mental and physical energy.

This class also practises such an imagination because of the external influ-ence of educational experts. Mrs Rich, like the other teachers at this school, has attended professional development sessions with a leader she clearly respects. Here is how she explains the role this leader has played.

> I need to say that this constant reflecting is probably due to [...]. She's worked at our school for many years, and we have her for two sessions, two days [per term] probably, to plan our units. But she has given us many, many strategies, and even just those ones I've mentioned: she encourages us to always reflect, always think, you know, get the children to have a journey. How far have you got, you know, what are you thinking about. And constantly question them about that. But her strategies encourage much thinking. Just the simple strategies 'think, pair, share'. So the usual children don't dominate, so every child has a voice, and there's many ways of doing that' (Catholic School, author interview with teacher, 11 September 2007).

## Teachers Variously Modelling Connection Making

If imagination is a form of connection making or thinking tool that can be purposefully taught, as Mrs Rich and VELS agree, and if this must be modelled by the teachers' own ways of thinking, then we face a question. Perhaps all people make connections between ideas – that is, 'think' in the same way. Then teachers will model the same processes, and children will learn to think in a similar manner. Or perhaps teachers make connections in different ways, and hence will model different ways of making connections. Then children in different classes and schools will learn to think differently. I am going to suggest that the second is the case, revealing teachers as modelling and validating very different ways of making connections between ideas. But there is more. If children are to learn new ways of making connections, surely teachers (and social scientists) can also be taught to make connections in new ways. What may be needed is to make old habits explicit and to think through their implications. This is what I attempt here.

If imagination is thought-made-explicit, then we have five patterns of imagining modelled at these five different schools. How might we value them? I will suggest that we pay close attention to Mrs Rich, the teacher who prioritises this mode of imagining in her teaching, and teaches thinking with multiple strategies and open-ended tasks. If we take seriously the mode of imagination as thinking, we find in Mrs Rich's class the most varied and ability-sensitive practice. It is most in tune with a relational metaphysics.

Let us look again across the five schools to ask how teachers model thinking, ending with Catholic School. We will open with two stories of linear connection making.

## BRIDGING GAPS

### Thinking at Independent School

In class at Independent School, connections are validated if they provide the correct answer to the problem posed. The process of thinking is the recall or identification of those connections that are correct while navigating around those that are incorrect. These are linear 'if ... then' forms of connection making. Mr Robertson will allow discussion for a short while until he states the answer he was expecting. This is the case when he reads to the class from *Toad Rage*, a children's book by Morris Gleitzman. He asks the children what they predict the humans are planning to do with the cane toad protagonists. The children suggest some possibilities, and Mr Robertson returns with 'You don't think they're going to use them to scare someone?' The class agrees with him that is most likely (Independent School, author field notes, 29 March 2007). Instead of using this as an opportunity to encourage divergent imaginative thinking, Mr Robertson claims both that there is a correct answer, and that he knows it.

Mathematics classes, too, generally follow the 'if ... then' structure. These lessons often start with Mr Robertson talking about a real world scenario, but this is used to help the children understand the problem, not to give the maths meaning in itself. These scenarios provide the content for the 'if'. One time, for example, Mr Robertson opens the lesson by getting children to imagine that he made sandwiches to sell at cricket games, doubling his money each day. How many days, he puts it to them, would it take to get one million dollars? Then, leaving the sandwiches scenario behind, he hands out sheets of paper, blank except for a series of squares for the answers found by doubling each previous answer. The point isn't to work out how much money Mr Robertson would have made with his sandwich venture, but to understand the concept of doubling well enough to write the correct answers on the sheet (Independent School, author field notes, 27 March 2007). The class spends many of the remaining mathematics lessons of my visit practising for the New South Wales mathematics competition. This likewise frames questions in real-world terms, then asks children to choose the correct multi-choice answer.

In story writing too, the children are directed in such a way as to make them negotiate their way to an original story within rules about what they should and must not do. Though they are free to choose the scenario, the 'if', the possible consequences, the 'thens', are limited. Children are told how they should structure their stories (Independent School, author field notes, 19 April 2007); given sentences they might and must not open their stories with (Independent School, author field notes, 16 April 2007); and told what they must not include (violence and Pokemon, in particular) (Independent School, author field notes, 28 March and 19 April 2007). Their thinking is to be original but only within stated bounds. A good story is one is that contains interesting words and permissible topics.

We see this use of imagination as thinking towards correct answers very clearly also in lessons about 'good' behaviour. One day a child brings chocolates to school and refuses to share them. Mr Robertson and the teacher from the class next door gather their children together. Mr Robertson says that 'You've got to ask why they're bringing them. Is it a power thing? Lording it over other people? We don't like that here'. After a little more talk from Mr Robertson and Mrs Merton, Mr Robertson continues to encourage the children to think about the behaviour of others, asking in such a way that the children know that there are right answers and a limited number of them. 'What are the four main things people are seeking when they misbehave?' Gradually, and with teacher direction, answers are suggested and distilled: 'attention'; 'vengeance'; 'power'; 'to make up for inadequacies'. Mr Robertson writes these on the board (Independent School, author field notes, 28 March 2007). This too works on an 'if … then' logic. If children are well behaved then they are not seeking these four things. If they are badly behaved then they are. The only thinking left for children to do is work out which of the four motives is the correct one.

This encourages children not to question, but to repeat assumptions. I see this clearly as I talk with two boys and the conversation turns to federal politics. These nine-year-olds disagree over who they want to win the federal election that will be held in six months' time. Miles wants Kevin Rudd to win. Neville says, 'No way. Howard should win,' but can't explain why. His mother is an economist, he tells me, and 'Australia doesn't have enough money to worry about global warming. Once we were rich, you know, like in the gold rush'. Miles disagrees. 'We should do wind. If Mr Howard does nuclear I will leave the country'. When I ask where he will go he becomes flustered and cross: he doesn't know the 'then' to that question (Independent School, author field notes, 26 March 2007). One politician is better than the other because of associations they have heard from mothers who are economists, and from circles that are anti-nuclear. These are examples of connection making that stress correctness through repetition of the answers given by others. It is a learning of associations: if this, then that.

## Thinking at Steiner School

In our class at Steiner School there is also a linear pattern of connection making, but instead of 'if ... then', the dominant pattern for connection making is by narrative. Connections are to be formed by validating only the strings that build sensible stories. We recall from chapter four that at this school everything is to be connected to the morning story, and meaning is to be built by encouraging the children's pictorial imaginations and warm feelings. Shirley tells me that most of her time in preparation is spent thinking 'how can I make this connec-tion' between the morning story and the lesson topic (Steiner School, author field notes, 6 June 2007).

We find this type of narrative connection making sanctioned also in the stories told to make sense of mathematics. This is very clear in the students' records of mathematics learning. In their large mathematics books they have all written the same series of stories linking the Norse myths to long division. The first book for the year has a title page 'Long Division in Valhalla', and a picture, similar in all, of a castle. The first task is to work out using addition in 'houses of numbers' how many seats would be needed for all the heroes, gods, and Valkyries at Odin's feast. The next page asks how Iduna might divide her apples among the gods, and the following page asks how runes might be divided. And so it goes on, each page referring to episodes in the morning story (Steiner School, author field notes, 17 June 2007). As the class does mathematics together on the board, Shirley activates these stories again; modelling sums worked through in 'houses of numbers' and division under 'Thor's hammer', and reminding the children to do likewise. Through repeatedly connecting mathematical division to the morning story, these problems are linked to wider meaning. This meaning comes from a story and the solution will be to allow the story to continue – gods seated, gods with apples. This structure makes mathematics a set of connections within narrative conventions. This is quite the opposite of mathematics at Independent School, where narrative was abandoned in favour of concept.

The import of this becomes clear when we see what types of connections children are not allowed to make during class time. All connection making is to make narrative sense. So, for example, Shirley actively discourages children to make connections by the sound of words. During discussion time when children are encouraged to share ideas, Shirley mentions that a girl in the class is sick with whooping cough. Someone asks how to pronounce that illness, and Fran asks 'Do hoops come out of your mouth?' Shirley looks right at her, and pointedly does not reply (Steiner School, author field notes, 19 June 2007).

Steiner children are also not allowed to make connections that link types of objects in non-causal ways. Shirley tells the class, again in discussion time, that assistant teacher Paul's washing machine is broken. A little later, Shirley praises the children for having had no warnings yet that week, saying that Paul might have to bake the cake he had promised for achieving a week without warnings. Presumably thinking about the broken washing machine, Morgan jokes, 'I hope his oven doesn't break too'. Shirley is sharp, replying 'I don't see how that could happen.' A couple of kids quietly suggest things, but this type of connection made between similar appliances has been de-legitimated (Steiner School, author field notes, 6 June 2007).

We find children reiterating narrative connection making in their own games. At this school children play imaginative games that are extremely complex. At Steiner School imaginative play and talk are achieved through the acting and speaking of stories. For example, over lunch one day a girl finds her jacket over in the corner near where the boys are sitting. She lays it down on the couch and says that they would have to get X-rays to find out exactly where the boy germs were located on it. Another girl comes over, miming and explaining that she has a box 'with three golden locks'. 'Put it down,' she is told, and the jacket is 'put in'. She takes the 'box' and walks to the edge of the mat. It is 'thrown to the bottom of the sea', but someone asks 'What if it gets washed ashore?' 'It's in Antarctica', they decide. The first girl picks up her jacket from where it has been lying all the time, and says 'It will have to be dry-cleaned. And I won't be able to wear it for about three weeks'. In this way she ends the game without breaking the narrative stream (Steiner School, author field notes, 8 June 2007).

This is a piece of child-directed talk in which we find narratives being woven together. The overall story remains throughout: that a jacket has become contaminated and needs to be dealt with. Narrative solutions are put forward, ushering in imaginative objects – X-rays and boxes locked with gold. Potential problems are suggested and solved in an ad hoc manner. The narrative ends where it started. The jacket is contaminated but can be dry-cleaned. These children show their skill at keeping a story together, even as its content diverges. They are exercising an impressive skill in making narrative connections.

## Foundational Knowing:
## The World as the Source of Stories to Tell and Answers to Find

These two ways of making connections – finding correct answers to problems by an 'if ... then' logic, and creating meaning through causal or narrative relations – are forms of linear connection making. Despite this similarity they are also very different. In one account, the world is ordered by what is told as 'factual' truth, and in the other, by 'narrative' truth. 'Factual truths' are seen to exist independent of any necessary connection to the scenario used to explain them. It does not matter whether Mr Robertson tells a story about making sandwiches at the cricket or quite another story; if you double sixteen then you will always get thirty-two. Narrative truths, on the other hand, are always connected to each other and to their telling. In either case, however, the next in the series is always already pointed to.

Additionally, these are both ways of foundational connection making: those that follow a logic of truth. They assume and enact the world as separate from those who know about it. Both apply their work to the gap that is seen to exist between knower and world. In the case of an 'if ... then' pattern, this gap is to be bridged by stipulating conditions of the world and asking knowers to suggest the logical consequences of these conditions. This bridges the gap by appealing to the contents of the knower's mind. This says, 'if the world is this way, then via a knower's own logic learnt as rules in class, the world must also be that way'. In the case of narrative connections, the gap between world and knower will be bridged similarly – if these events, then those events. This time, however, the ontological status of the world is different. Instead of claiming to tell true things, narrative connections claim to tell useful allegories of the world. This is to doubt that we can ever really bridge the gap between knower and world. Instead we are limited to telling stories that give some allegorical representation of what the world is really like.

The core difference, then, between the two ways of making linear connections is in the ontology each reinforces. Both patterns of connection making share a foundationalist premise, positing that there is a world we all share. The first assumes that we can reason about the world, while the other suggests that we have to move through earlier human attempts to give it shape and meaning before we can start to grasp it. This is a difference between what might be called scientific empiricism and cultural relativism. Factual 'if ... then' logic assumes we can make deductions from what is observed. Narrative 'if ... then' logic suggests we can have a sense of the meaning of things but never really know. This opposes the empiricism of the Enlightenment with the 'thinking into' of Vico and the counter-Enlightenment (Berlin 1976; see also chapter six).

A quite different model can be extracted from the connection making favoured at Special School and Government School. There we find connection making as the building of sets.

## THINKING AS MAKING SETS

### Thinking at Special School

The focus in the class at Special School, a school for low-IQ students, is to teach children to appropriately group concrete objects. Good thinking here is understood to be making connections between like objects, and putting them into the appropriate general categories. Teachers model this pattern for children to imitate as they learn to use the computer program 'Kahootz'. This program lets users build a scene by choosing a background and adding appropriate objects. These can then be animated, and users can navigate around the scene, looking at it from different angles. This program teaches many skills in using computers and provides children with experience in visualising things from different perspectives. The skill that assistant teacher Michaela stresses though, especially at the start of a new project, is choosing objects appropriate to the scene.

She talks the class through this: that term their project is going to be about the seasons. The current season is spring, so, she asks, what would they put in their scenes? What objects fit in the category of spring? Underneath she writes what they say in a column, sometimes adding a row when objects belong to the same category:

- Grass
- Roads
- Concrete
- Flowers – roses, sunflowers
- Plants – trees
- Hills

When they stop suggesting new ideas, she asks them, 'What happens to the animals in spring?' 'They have babies,' the children reply, and they list some – kittens, puppies, lambs. The bell rings for lunch, but before she lets them go, Michaela says of their Kahootz scenes, 'Everyone must do the same, there's no trains, there's no bicycles, there's no cars'. These, she is saying, would be inappropriate objects in the category 'spring' (Special School, author field notes, 9 October 2007).

They use this program one afternoon a week, and Michaela is strict in giving approval to some objects and not others. The children know that there are rules about what 'fit' but they are unsure of exactly what these rules are. Victor asks if he could put bees into the scene: do bees like flowers? Michaela says yes, and that there could be birds too. Birds also like spring flowers (Special School, author field notes, 9 October 2007). Dwayne puts a giant fish in his. Michaela deletes it, saying firmly that it has nothing to do with a spring garden (Special School, author field notes, 16 October 2007).

It is easy to find other examples that also support the idea that thinking at Special School is predominately about making the correct categories of concrete nouns. On one occasion, the class are completing a sheet, filling in the appropriate words for the openings 'today is ____. The weather is ____.' Logan is told off first for drawing a picture of the sun when it is raining outside, and then for drawing a train. First he chooses the wrong word from the right set, then a word from the wrong set entirely. Senior teacher Diane tells him, 'Stop. It doesn't say anything about a train so we shouldn't have a picture of a train' (Special School, author field notes, 9 October 2007). On another occasion, the children very gleefully mix up the words that describe the day, month, and season on the board. Now they read as nonsense, 'Today is spring, tomorrow will be November'. What they are enjoying is breaking the rules of each set. Michaela makes them fix it up, and tells them off. 'Not funny' (Special School, author field notes, 19 October 2007).

At first sight it may seem that making groups of concrete objects as part of general categories has little to do with imagination. This impression is countered by the fact that children are told to imagine the scene 'spring' before they start listing objects that fit into the scene. It is by moving between imaginary ground (spring scene) and figures (grass, lambs, hills) that they are able to do this task.

This is not the only way to connect the world in imagination so that sets are made.

## Thinking at Government School

In our classroom at Government School, children are inducted into a thinking pattern based on sign systems, particularly the systems of language and symbols. This comes from, and re-enacts, an understanding of the world in which everything is 'embedded' in time and place. These form sets that, while perhaps logically arbitrary, make sense in terms of the wider social world. Children at Government School are to learn to think about and behave in a world governed by a system of rights and responsibilities (Government School, author field notes, 30 May 2007). They are to learn that other people have different perspectives, and, as they put together timelines from an 'Aboriginal perspective', that even historical time can be systematised differently (Government School, author field notes, 24 May 2007). They learn how to read the words and the illustrations of books as revealing a sign system quite different from how it is now. As they compare the present and past, they talk about changes in specific systems (Government School, author field notes, 24 May 2007). These are all ways of making sets of culturally connected objects, teaching that different cultures and different times are guided by different conventional sets of meaning.

This is evident in how Justine encourages her class to think as she reads to them from the book *My Place*. One day she asks children to look at the picture and think about what has changed since the book opened on pre-contact Aboriginal time. They talk about the river having become more 'sludgy' and 'harder to find'; the clothes and the buildings 'becoming more advanced, the buildings looking more like buildings and the clothes more like clothes'. In doing so, they are simultaneously comparing the systems shown in the picture of the 1870s (rivers, clothes, buildings) with those shown on the pre-contact Aboriginal page, and also with what they know of the present (Government School, author field notes, 24 May 2007). When Tom shows me the picture he has drawn this is the sign system he points out: Scots (shown by their wearing kilts), Chinese (in conical hats), and Aussies. 'How can you tell they're Aussies?' I ask. This is clear, apparently, by their bowler hats (Government School, author field notes, 23 May 2007). These clothes are to designate members of nationality sets.

This class has been doing a unit about multicultural Australia and its history. When Justine suggests they make bookmarks to thank the student teachers who have been coming in for literacy, the children suggest drawing various things that symbolise multicultural Australia's history. These range from the Australian flag, to symbols of peace, to flags of the different places Australians have migrated from. Justine compliments the variety of these ideas, saying 'for me it was just a seed of an idea and you're making sense of it'. Sense is making the set of appropriate signs (Government School, author field notes, 24 May 2007). When completed, most bookmarks refer to the sign systems of multicultural Australia. One group has done three symbols of Australia over time: an Aboriginal woman sitting, gold-mining tools, and a convict ship. Another has done lots of small symbols: flags and mining picks, and Chinese dragons, and dot paintings.

The children are also adept at using sign systems in their conversations. On one occasion children are talking about the system of shapes in relation to eyes. After one child says she has stayed up late playing computer games, another pretends to be an adult and warns 'You'll get square eyes'. Another suggests, 'Imagine if you actually did get square eyes', and the others start listing different shaped eyes: triangle eyes, hexagon eyes, semicircle eyes (Government School, author field notes, 22 May 2007). This is verbal play connecting the system of shapes to the culturally meaningful phrase 'square eyes'.

## Relative Knowing: Sign Systems as the Ground for Set Making

In both these classrooms, connections are made as groups of figures relevant to some stipulated ground. This is connection making as making sets. Imagination in these cases means expanding the list of possible members of a set. This is a way of thinking in which it can be clearly determined what is a legitimate and what is an illegitimate member by referral to the ground or collecting concept. Trains are not legitimate in the group of facts about the day; convict ships are legitimate in the group of symbols of Australian history. But while each stipulates legitimacy, neither limits the number of possible answers. There are many possible members of each set, and creative connection making might bring many of these out. Here then is potential for multiple correct answers.

Again, however, the stories of these two classrooms also reveal differences in the ontology animating their connection making, and this rests on a division between nature-made and human-made. At Special School collecting categories are about the natural world. Into these spring scenes and accounts of the weather only 'real' objects fit. These sets should accurately represent the world as it is – no sun when it is raining, no fish in a garden. And they should only show things that are 'natural' to the scene. There are to be no trains, bicycles, or cars in a spring garden, although in an actual spring garden there certainly could be. As is perhaps appropriate for these low-IQ children, these are sets that simplify and order.

At Government School the collecting concepts are from human life and history, and thus it is not surprising that human objects are allowable. But moreover, it is clear that human choice has determined just what are appropriate objects for each category. It was humans who put convict ships into the history of Australia, and humans from China who chose to wear conical hats in the past.

I have highlighted the differences between these four ways of making connections, arguing that two are directed towards making linear patterns of thought while the other two make sets. I have also distinguished between each pair, suggesting that at Independent and Special Schools, connection making practices claim reality for the natural world only, while at Steiner and Government Schools reality is claimed for how humans have understood and given meaning to the world. But, in fact, all four have something in common. They all make a separation between nature and culture. To explain, I turn to Bruno Latour.

## THINKING AS PURIFICATION

In *We Have Never Been Modern*, Latour argues that modernity has appeared to be a solid achievement because of the way modern people are used to organising information. In his picture, the world is always made up of complex webs linking actors and objects in entangled ways. Modernity has been based on the pretence that these webs can be neatly sorted out, dividing the world into separate categories of nature and culture. He calls this purification. This, however useful it is, crucially misrepresents the world according to Latour. More, much of the time we actually live comfortably with the entangled networks. This is why, despite our efforts, we have never been modern (Latour 1993).

This separating is analogous to the work of primary school teachers. We have seen that at Steiner School connection making is done through narrative links. This is akin to saying that we grasp the natural world through the attempts of earlier people and their stories that made sense of it. This is to lay a cultural lens over children's experiences of the natural, separating nature and culture by giving primacy to the cultural (this is done in turn to make children give an enhanced emotional response to the natural). At Independent School, by contrast, nature and culture are again separated, but now stories about culturally sensible 'real world scenarios' are used to provide a context for the natural to make sense. Here, nature and culture are kept apart by the primacy placed on the natural as the 'true'.

As I have indicated above, the classes that make connections as sets are also engaged in separating nature and culture. The separation is more straightforward in these classes, with groups being made of either natural or cultural entities. At Special School, categories are made that will contain only natural objects within natural scenes and will refuse unnatural objects as inappropriate: neither fish nor trains belong in gardens. At Government School, the categories are understood as being primarily social in their origins and all objects are members of sets by social convention. This could admit to complex networks of nature-culture, but only if these were a reiteration of how people are told as already understanding the world: only if those webs were already 'really' cultural.

What would it look like for a teacher to encourage their students to think with a relational logic? Separations are not a priori made between nature and culture, the worlds 'out there', and 'in here'. Knowers are understood as participants in the world, and their knowledge is that which helps them participate. We turn again to Mrs Rich to see how this might look in practice.

## Thinking as Making Relational Webs

Recall the story we opened this conclusion with. There we see Mrs Rich playing a song for the children to think about. Dividing the possible responses into a Y-chart, Mrs Rich instructs children to listen carefully and be ready to share their imaginative experiences of what the place in the song looks like, sounds like, and feels like. This Y-chart does not ask for a splitting of nature from culture.

This activity asks children to call up in their imaginations a mixture of the empirical and the emotional effects of the song. What do they 'see' by listening to the song? What do they 'hear'? These are questions that require children to form imaginaries through the words and music they hear. These could be of natural or human made objects. 'What did you feel?' on the other hand asks children to reflect on the emotions the song called up. This asks them about how they imagine it would be to live, to be a social human, in that house, and its surrounds.

And children's responses do not distinguish between natural and cultural. What they hear are birds, breezes, barbecues, and twenty years ago. What they feel is cold, old homes and the loneliness of having few visitors. Mrs Rich does not claim any answers are more correct than others, but she does encourage new suggestions: 'Anything different?' She is open to surprise – she had thought it a happy song. In this way, the task remains open-ended and any suggestion that connects to the song welcomed. These could include connecting this song to another text, to the self, and one's experience, or to other things of the world. These are truly a mixing of the natural and the cultural, an invitation for making webs. Keeping together the natural and the cultural, and hence world and knowers, it is enacting a relational metaphysics.

## CONCLUSION: CONNECTIONS AND SEPARATIONS

What I have tried to do in this conclusion is follow a paraphrased version of Mrs Rich's insistence that 'good listeners make connections'. Good ethnographers, I suggest, also make connections. This is a part of the imagination we too should bring to work. The connections I have made are between different classroom practices and the thinking patterns embedded in them. More, and again, following Mrs Rich's insistence that imaginative thinking be made explicit, I have tried to visualise these patterns in terms of lines, sets, and webs.

In order to make these connections I have had to make separations. I have separated classrooms with linear from those with set-making thinking patterns. I have separated those that give primacy to nature from those that give primacy to culture. And I have separated teachers who work to keep nature and culture apart from that one teacher who works to keep nature and culture enmeshed.

I have also connected these to the work of scholars such as Bruno Latour. He told us that our belief in our own modernity has been based on a false premise. Instead of always working to separate nature from culture, as moderns have done, we should accept that we live in a world where nature and culture are entangled. We should learn to think – and act and assign value – in ways that keep them together.

This conclusion has been an exercise in an imagination prevalent in academic work – making explicit our patterns of making connections and separations, concepts, and categories. But, I would suggest, we are seldom aware of the choices we make about the patterns of thought we use. I hope that showing the choices teachers have inadvertently made might help readers become more aware of how they can think and imagine differently.

# AFTERWORD

ONE CONSEQUENCE OF TAKING MULTIPLICITY SERIOUSLY IS THAT CONCLUD-
ing becomes difficult in new ways. If, as I have argued, imagination is multiple
because practised or performed in different ways, and if these performances are
ongoing and potentially ever changing, what can be said to 'tie it together', 'wrap
it up', or 'give the last word'? This is a problem that Annemarie Mol acknowledges
in her 2002 book *The Body Multiple.* She lessens its brunt by calling her final
chapter simply 'Chapter 6: Doing Theory'. She spends this chapter in thinking
through the ways her account of multiple atherosclerosis might interfere with
contemporary practices of science, medicine, philosophy, and social science,
and beyond. In this way, she sidesteps the need for too much 'tying up' and she
can leave readers with the picture of different atheroscleroses that sometimes
co-exist, mutually include, tensely include, and interfere with one another (Mol
2002: 151–184).

Mol's multiplicity interacts in these ways because she works in one site,
a particular hospital, and atherosclerosis is carried between departments by
human bodies. What she is interested in is how atherosclerosis in one part of
the hospital can be both different from, and yet fit together with, atherosclerosis in another.

My multiplicity shares this problem to some extent. These five imaginations I
see in practice happen to greater or lesser extent at each of these schools – along
with others too. They meet in classroom practice and also here in this book.
But instead of wondering how multiple performances come together in practice
I wonder how they can be theorised as related but separate. My solution is to
extend the imagery we use to think about multiplicity.

## *Images of Gathering*

For my work there are various ways of gathering together multiplicity. I will describe these through the figures of the umbrella, the fence, and the braided river.

An umbrella is a collection of spokes that come together at the top in one common node. Using the umbrella image for dealing with multiplicity we would work to find the common ancestor, the cause of the family resemblance. In this case we would ask, as White (1990), Warnock (1976), McGinn (2004), and others have done, what do all these imaginations have in common? What does this tell us about what imagination is, really? This is to imagine that all imaginations are deviations from the pure form, poor copies of the original. The umbrella image for doing conclusions, then, draws us into a Platonic discourse of model and copy. We would ask which – of performing oneself as imaginative, representing the world in minds, thinking of otherness, making relationships or making connections – is closest to being the real imagination.

An alternative that has been popular at least since Wittgenstein's later works has been to imagine conclusions as a fence. The fence image I am using is that of a series of posts standing in a row. Each imagination, this would say, bears a resemblance, but now we are not interested in the ancestor but only in the sameness and differences between siblings. Using the fence image for doing conclusions we rest in difference, stuck with the static and separate. Different imaginations are different, we would say, and they will (or should) remain different.

The final option I will present here is one I will image with the braided river (talking in terms of flows comes from the work of Mol and Law 1994; Mol and de Laet 2000; and Pickering 2008). The South Island of New Zealand has a range of mountains like a spine running up its length. At one point the rivers that flow from this mountain range run over a large flat plain, the Canterbury Plain. Through this area the rivers run wide, many channels of water flowing separately for long distances before joining together again. The bridges that span these rivers are lengthy, a challenge for children convinced that good luck will come to she who can hold her breath for their entire span. After floods, the stones that divide the water have moved and the channels are aligned differently. To understand the flows of water would require taking account of the water, the stones, the contours of the land, the tree trunks that are washed down from the upper forests, the placement of bridge struts, the paths made by thirsty stock animals, and the history of flood and drought.

Using the braided river to image the gathering work that endings are supposed to do allows us to talk about how things are done differently – but, given the many other elements in play, to not assume that they will or should remain separate. Water flows come together and separate along the course of the river, and over time they merge and realign. Their particular separateness at a given time depends on the accommodations and resistances of stones and tree trunks, bridges, and stock animals (Pickering 1995). Likewise, imaginations are being done differently in the classrooms I write about, but they may not remain as they are, or even remain separate from each other.

To follow the flows we would have to find some way to name them, to label them as particular. Whatever label we choose would be a tool allowing us to recognise each flow as distinct but able to be merged again with others. This is what we do when we name imaginations we see in classrooms and follow their movements.

To use the braided river image for an ending we would be able to talk about the resistances and accommodations—including the histories of those—that make teachers do imagination differently in their classrooms. But we wouldn't be forced to say that their imaginations are always kept distinct and separate. The needs of students, the policies of schools, fashions in educational theory, curriculum and politics, and experiences of teachers, all are subject to ongoing change. In the time I write, each imagination was stable enough to be recognisable as an individual stream. But the imaginations teachers are doing can and probably will change. During each school day teachers did imagination in various ways. Maybe over time teachers will come closer to doing one or other of the imaginations I have described here, or maybe to others I have not. Over the course of a school day, or a school year, or on return after the holidays, these changes might be great enough to see teachers' practices of imagination form an entirely new stream or to merge with an existing one.

## Generative Concepts: Who

I have said that part of the job of endings is to gather and summarise. This is what I have been writing about as I write about the images umbrella, fence, and braided river. These are all ways of imaging possible ways of collecting up. I have associated the umbrella image with the belief that there is one real imagination, its true form, and that multiplicity comes from a deviation from that form. The fence image I have associated with the Wittgensteinian notion of family resemblance – things that are related but different. And the braided river I have used to image differences that are achieved in relation to the surroundings and that change course, that connect, and separate in new ways as the surrounding relations change.

But gathering is only one part of what endings generally do. Another one of their jobs is to be explicit about what writers intend for readers to walk away with. These are the ideas that writers hope might 'travel'. For some scholars such as Mol, Star, and Sørensen, the question of how well ideas travel is intended to replace the belief in the primacy of 'truth'. The argument runs thus: we don't live in a foundational world where the aim is to represent the real, but in one where knowledge is more or less useful, more or less good at becoming related to other things. In a relational world truth is not a particularly useful ideal – things seem true when they are good at relating to material entities. This is not to suggest that what I have said here is not true – the stories I have told certainly did happen in classrooms. What I want, though, is to move beyond truth and to wonder about how well my analysis moves into new relations across time and space. This is to talk about how well they interfere or how well they travel.

The question, then, for doing this afterword is about which concepts I hope might travel well. I have two types of answer. One concerns the information contained in this book. Under this heading we might think of the ideas I have written about, and which readers might share with others in their own writing, in conversation, or in teaching. To me these include ways of thinking about the foundational and relational, the stories of classrooms, and the five ways of doing imagination – as telling a good yarn, imagining oneself other, forming pictures in the mind, having a friend, making connections. I hope these are important ideas, and I hope that readers will find them useful and interesting to talk and write about. Readers will, I hope, also find bits that, for their own reasons, they set into motion.

But there is a second way in which I hope the concepts in this book might travel. I borrow this idea from the writing of Donna Haraway, who uses figures like the cyborg and the modest witness to provide models of what she regards as good actors (see Haraway 1991; 1997). For Haraway these are the type of actors necessary to the science that she hopes for. Her figures are able to know and act in new and ethical ways. I have also written about figures able to know and act in ethical ways, but they give a less science-fiction first impression. My figures are ideal instantiations, making complete the tendencies I have watched in real people and felt in myself.

I have presented two such figures. One masquerades as myself, though she is rid of many of my confusions and is consistent in her actions. She is the ethnographer I aspire to be more than the ethnographer I am. She struggles to be aware of the imagination she is using as she does her work. She notices how these affect what she is able to see and write about, and how she is able to understand. She learns to notice these imaginations from the work of primary school teachers. From one, Shirley, she learnt to notice her own representational practices. With another, Justine, she learnt to imagine herself other, and from Mr Robertson, she became aware of presenting herself as creative. From Diane, Michaela, and their colleagues, she realised the value in thinking and imagining with others, and with Mrs Rich she pushed herself to make patterns of thinking explicit. She hopes that other ethnographers might think of her as something akin to one of their ethnographic subjects, someone to learn to think with.

I also wrote about the relational teacher. She is a figure that all teachers embody to a greater or lesser extent. She is responsive to student need and flexible enough in her teaching practice to shift her lessons, while still retaining an overall picture of what she wants her students to achieve. Each teacher had an overall picture of what imagination she wanted her children to be able to do – and this depended on her own biography and on her students' needs and parents' wishes, as well as more the institutional requirements of school and curriculum. These varied from the need to form pictures in one's mind, to present oneself as imaginative, to think oneself other, to be friends, and to make connections. Some, however, were better than others at broadening their intentions as student interest and need wavered. I credit Justine, Michaela, and Mrs Rich in particular as doing work that resonates with this figure.

## Ending the Ending: Futures

I have gathered the five imaginations with the image of the braided river. I have given some 'take-home messages' for ethnographers and teachers: figures that act in what I believe are 'good' ways. What about for readers who are not, or not only, interested in theory or in good ethnography and teaching? What about for readers more broadly interested in children and imagination? In the end, as I used Shirley's words to say at the beginning, what seems to matter about imagination are the futures our performances make possible. What about the challenges that imagination is called upon to solve?

Each teacher I worked with had at least an implicit vision of the future, and for each teacher, their students' ability to imagine would partially determine their success there. For Shirley (chapter four), the hope is for children to be able to think in wholly new ways and able therefore to find paths out of our current and future collective crises. For Mr Robertson (chapter five), it is a future in which some students are succeeding in impressing others through their presentation of themselves as humorous. For Justine (chapter six), it is a future riddled with personal traumas that children are able to mitigate and negotiate through their ability to imagine themselves other. For Diane and Michaela (chapter seven), the vision is of children able to bond with others in the mainstream community despite their intellectual disadvantages. And for Mrs Rich (concluding chapter), the vision is of self-reflective individuals good at thinking and thinking about how they think.

These are some possible futures and possible future humans. There are multiple others, and multiple potential ways of performing imagination for 'the future'.

From each teacher I learnt something about an entity that we might call the *relational imagination*. This should be thought of as something to aim towards in our practices, including our ethnographic practices. From some teachers we learnt about imagining together. Among other things, this is a matter of finding ways to imagine ourselves as particular types of group, cooperative more than competitive, with shared goals (see chapter seven). For this to work well we need to notice difference as well as sameness, and accept that our intentions need to be broad enough to withstand a certain amount of mangling (chapter six). We need always to focus on making connections in our thinking, being able to recognise and make more complex patterns than just lines and sets (chapter eight). Doing all these things successfully will require discipline as well as humour (chapter five) and we will have to keep in sight that we are intervening even when we represent (chapter four). It is my belief that we should work towards doing this type of imagination for our future possibilities for good knowing and good living, stuck as we are in our classed and classing bodies. We might aim to embody this new figure: the relational imaginer.

My question has always been about what to do next. How can we use imagination to solve our public problems? What do we want our children to be able to do for their – and our – future? In a way this takes us back to the teaching imagination, to ask simultaneously about the imagination we want children to be able to do and the imaginative habits we might use to support this. Key, I think, is recognising what I assert from the start: that imagination is something we *do* and that we do in relation to the people, words, objects, and environments we are surrounded with. Noticing our surroundings, and noticing what is made possible with these, is a start. Moreover, when we recognise that imagination is material and relational, then we notice that it can be done differently: in multiple – though not just any – ways. Giving children tools to be able to notice and do different imaginations, and to notice that different imaginations might be useful given different surroundings, is a second move. This means helping children to become flexible and responsive imaginers. And third, what I think is so powerful about imagination in human life is that it gives us an ability to generate new things. These don't have to be massively innovative, or hugely powerful, or wildly creative to be important. Finding a popular way to present oneself, or a surprising way to visualise a problem, or to make a new relationship, or to tell a good story: all these are important. We should value newness even in its most simple forms. Newness can be as simple and difficult as putting two things together that used to be apart so that people don't have to switch between. Newness can be as simple and difficult as finding ways to play together and work together and think together so that we can go on into the future more together than we were.

# BIBLIOGRAPHY

## PRIMARY SOURCES

Australian Bureau of Statistics, 'Census Data', 2006, <http://www.abs.gov.au/ websitedbs/ D3310114.nsf/home/Census+data> [accessed 6 October 2008]

Rood, D., 'Steiner Program for State Schools', *The Age* (4 October 2006), p. 11

Rout, M., 'Hard Questions Asked on Steiner's Spiritual Classroom', *The Weekend Australian*, 28.29 (2007), p. 3

Saulwick, I., and D. Muller,. 'What Parents Want from their Children's Education in Independent Schools: Condensed Report' [Report by Association of Independent Schools of Victoria Incorporated: Melbourne, 1999]

'Thrass: For Phonetics Teaching and ESL', <http://www.thrass.com.au> [accessed June 2007]

Victorian Curriculum and Assessment Authority, 'Victorian Essential Learning Standards, Home', 2006, < http://vels.vcaa.vic.edu.au> [accessed throughout 2007–2008]

—— 'Victorian Essential Learning Standards: Overview' [Victorian Department of Education and Training Booklet, 2005]

—— 'Blueprint for Government Schools: Future Directions for Education in the Victorian Government School Sector', 2004a

—— 'Introducing the Victorian Essential Learning Standards', 2004b

Victorian Curriculum and Assessment Authority, 'Curriculum Standards Framework: Home', 2002, <http://csf.vcaa.vic.edu.au> [accessed throughout 2008–2008]

## SECONDARY SOURCES

Addelson, K. P., *Moral Passages: Toward a Collectivist Moral Theory* (New York: Routledge, 1994)

—— 'Knowers/Doers and their Moral Problems', *Feminist Epistemologies* (New York and London: Routledge, 1993), pp. 265–294

—— *Impure Thoughts: Essays on Philosophy, Feminism, and Ethics* (Philadelphia: Temple University Press, 1991)

Addelson, K. P., and E. Potter, 'Making Knowledge', in K. P. Addelson, ed., *Impure Thoughts: Essays on Philosophy, Feminism, and Ethics* (Philadelphia: Temple University Press, 1991), pp. 221–238

Adkins, L., and C. Lury, 'Introduction: What is the Empirical?', *European Journal of Social Theory*, 12.1 (2009), 5–20

Alcoff, L., and E. Potter, eds, *Feminist Epistemologies* (New York and London: Routledge, 1993)

Althusser, L., *Lenin and Philosophy and Other Essays*, B. Brewster, trans. (London: NLB, 1977)

Arnold, R., *Empathic Intelligence: Teaching, Learning, Relating* (Sydney: University of New South Wales Press, 2005)

Ashmore, M., *The Reflexive Thesis: Wrighting Sociology of Scientific Knowledge* (Cambridge: Cambridge University Press, 1989)

Bakhtin, M., *The Dialogic Imagination*, M. Holquist. ed., M. Holquist, and C. Emerson, trans. (Austin and London: University of Texas Press, 1981)

Bateson, G., 'The Message "This is Play"', in R. E. Herron, and B. Sutton-Smith, eds, *Child's Play* (New York: John Wiley & Sons, 1971), pp. 261–269

Barcan, A., 'Educational Revolutions, Left, Right and Centre', *Quadrant*, 51.2 (2007), 24–34

Benjaminsen, N., 'Circulation of Authorizations – Authority as a Material and Processual Configuration', paper presented at EASST/4S Conference, Rotterdam (2008)

Berlin, I., *Vico and Herder: Two Studies in the History of Ideas* (London: Hogarth, 1976)

Bernstein, B., *Class, Codes and Control*, Vol. 3 (London: Routledge and K. Paul, 1975)

Briskman, L., 'Creative Product and Creative Process in Science and Art', in D. Dutton, and M. Krausz, eds, *The Concept of Creativity in Science and Art* (The Hague: Martinus Nijhoff Publishers, 1981)

Bourdieu, P., *Distinction: A Social Critique of the Judgement of Taste*, R. Nice, trans. (Cambridge, MA: Harvard University Press, 1984)

Bowker, G., and S. Leigh Star, *Sorting Things Out: Classification and its Consequences* (Cambridge, MA and London: MIT Press, 1999)

Burman, E., *Deconstructing Developmental Psychology* (London and New York: Routledge, 1994)

Butler, J., 'Conscience Doth Make Subjects of Us All', *Yale French Studies*, 88 (1995), 6–26

Callon, M., ed., *The Laws of the Markets* (London: Wiley–Blackwell, 1998)

Carter, R., *Language and Creativity: The Art of Common Talk* (London and New York: Routledge, 2004)

Castoriadis, C., *World in Fragments: Writings on Politics, Society, Psychoanalysis, and the Imagination*, D. A. Curtis, trans. (Stanford: Stanford University Press, 1997)

Charmaz, K., 'Grounded Theory: Objectivist and Constructivist Methods', in N. Denzin, and Y. Lincoln, eds, *Handbook of Qualitative Research*, 2nd edn (Thousand Oaks, CA: Sage, 2000), pp. 509–535

Cherednichenko, B. F., 'A Social Analysis of the Teaching of Thinking Skills in Victorian Primary Schools 1993–1996' (PhD thesis, University of Melbourne, 2000)

Code, L., *Rhetorical Spaces: Essays on Gendered Locations* (New York and London: Routledge, 1995)

Cropley, A., *More Ways than One: Fostering Creativity* (Norwood, NJ: Ablex, 1992)

Currie, G., and I. Ravenscroft, *Recreative Minds: Imagination in Philosophy and Psychology* (Oxford: Clarendon Press, 2002)

Diamond, C., *The Realistic Spirit: Wittgenstein, Philosophy, and the Mind* (Cambridge, MA: MIT Press, 1991)

Deleuze, G., *The Deleuze Reader*, C. V. Boundas, trans. (New York: Columbia University Press, 1993)

Dillon, M. C., *Merleau-Ponty's Ontology*, 2nd edn (Evanston, IL: Northwestern University Press, 1997)

Egan, K., *Getting it Wrong from the Beginning: Our Progressivist Inheritance from Herbert Spencer, John Dewey, and Jean Piaget* (New Haven, CT: Yale University Press, 2002)

—— *The Educated Mind: How Cognitive Tools Shape our Understanding* (Chicago and London: University of Chicago Press, 1997)

—— *Imagination in Teaching and Learning: Ages 8–15* (London: Routledge, 1992)

—— *Romantic Understanding: The Development of Rationality and Imagination, Ages 8–15* (New York: Routledge, 1990)

Feldman, D., M. Csikszentmihalyi, and H. Gardner, *Changing the World: A Framework for the Study of Creativity* (Westport, CT and London: Praeger, 1994)

Frawley, W., *Vygotsky and Cognitive Science: Language and the Unification of the Social and Computational Mind* (Cambridge, MA and London: Harvard University Press, 1997)

Gane, N., 'Concepts and the "New" Empiricism', *European Journal of Social Theory*, 12.1 (2009), 83–97

Gell, A., *Art and Agency: An Anthropological Theory* (Oxford: Clarendon Press, 1998)

Greene, M., *Releasing the Imagination: Essays on Education, the Arts, and Social Change* (San Francisco: Jossey-Bass, 1995)

Goldman, L., *Child's Play: Myth, Mimesis and Make-Believe* (Oxford and New York: Berg, 1998)

Hacking, I., *Representing and Intervening: Introductory Topics in the Philosophy of Natural Science* (Cambridge and New York: Cambridge University Press, 1983)

Hallinan, M., 'Introduction: Sociology of Education at the Threshold of the Twenty-first Century', in M. Hallinan, ed., *Handbook of the Sociology of Education* (New York: Klumer Academic and Plenum Publishers, 2000), pp. 1–12

Hallpike, C., *Foundations of Primitive Thought* (Oxford: Clarendon Press, 1979)

Haraway, D., 'Situated Knowledges and the Problem of Partial Perspectives', in S. Harding, ed., *The Feminist Standpoint Theory Reader: Intellectual and Political Controversies* (New York and London: Routledge, 2004), pp. 81–101

—— *How like a Leaf: An Interview with Thyrza Nichols Goodeve* (New York and London: Routledge, 2000)

—— *Modest_Witness@Second_Millenium.FemaleMan©_Meets_OncoMouse™: Feminism and Technoscience* (New York and London: Routledge, 1997)

—— 'A Game of Cat's Cradle: Science Studies, Feminist Theory, Cultural Studies', *Configurations*, 2.1 (1994), 59–71

—— *Simians, Cyborgs, and Women: The Reinvention of Nature* (London: Free Association Books, 1991)

Harding, S., 'Rethinking Standpoint Epistemology: What is "Strong Objectivity"?', in S. Harding, ed., *The Feminist Standpoint Theory Reader: Intellectual and Political Controversies* (New York and London: Routledge, 2004), pp. 127–140

Harwood, A. C., *The Recovery of Man in Childhood: A Study in the Educational Work of Rudolf Steiner* (London: Hodder and Stoughton, 1958)

Hastrup, K., and K. Fog Olwig, 'Introduction', in K. Hastrup, and K. Fog Olwig, eds, *Siting Culture: The Shifting Anthropological Object* (London and New York: Routledge, 1994), pp. 1–14

Hersch, E., 'Imagination and its Pathologies: Domain of the Unreal or a Fundamental Dimension of Human Reality?', in J. Phillips, and J. Morley, eds, *Imagination and its Pathologies* (Cambridge, MA and London: MIT Press, 2003), pp. 37–50

Holmes, D., *Integral Europe: Fast-Capitalism, Multiculturalism, Neofascism* (Princeton, NJ: Princeton University Press, 2000)

Holquist, M., 'Introduction', in M. Holquist, ed., M. Holquist, and C. Emerson, trans., *The Dialogic Imagination* (Austin and London: University of Texas Press, 1981), pp. xv–xxxiv

Hutchins, E., *Cognition in the Wild* (Cambridge, MA and London: MIT Press, 1995)

Kapferer, B., 'Anthropology and the Dialectic of the Enlightenment', *Australian Journal of Anthropology*, 18.1 (2007), 72–94

Kant, I., *Critique of Pure Reason*, N. Kemp Smith, trans. (London: Macmillan, 1929)

Kaufman, J., and R. Sternberg, eds, *The International Handbook of Creativity* (Cambridge: Cambridge University Press, 2006)

Khatena, J., and N. Khatena, *Developing Creative Talent in Art: A Guide for Parents and Teachers* (Stamford, CT: Ablex Publishing Corporation, 1999)

Kitchener, R., *Piaget's Theory of Knowledge: Genetic Epistemology and Scientific Reason* (New Haven, CT: Yale University Press, 1986)

Krausz, M., 'Creating and Becoming', in D. Dutton, and M. Krausz, eds, *The Concept of Creativity in Science and Art* (The Hague: Martinus Nijhoff Publishers, 1981), pp. 187–200

Koestler, A., 'The Three Domains of Creativity', in D. Dutton, and M. Krausz, eds, *The Concept of Creativity in Science and Art* (The Hague: Martinus Nijhoff Publishers, 1981), pp. 1–17

Kosslyn, S., *Image and Brain: The Resolution of the Imagery Debate* (Cambridge, MA and London: MIT Press, 1994)

Lakoff, G., and M. Johnson, *Metaphors We Live By* (Chicago and London: University of Chicago Press, 1980)

Latour, B., *Reassembling the Social: An Introduction to Actor-Network-Theory* (Oxford and New York: Oxford University Press, 2005)

—— *We Have Never Been Modern*, C. Porter, trans. (Cambridge, MA: Harvard University Press, 1993)

—— 'The Politics of Explanation: An Alternative', in S. Woolgar, ed., *Knowledge and Reflexivity: New Frontiers in the Sociology of Knowledge* (London: Sage, 1988), pp. 155–176

Lave, J., *Cognition in Practice* (Cambridge: Cambridge University Press, 1988)

Law, J., and M. Lien, 'Slippery: Fieldnotes in Empirical Ontology', *Social Studies of Science*, 43.3 (2012), 363–378

Law, J., 'Pinboards and Books: Juxtaposing, Learning and Materiality', in D. Kritt, and L. Winegar, eds, *Education and Technology: Critical Perspectives, Possible Futures* (Lanham: Lexington Books, 2007), pp. 125–149

—— *After Method: Mess in Social Science Research* (London and New York: Routledge, 2004)

—— *Aircraft Stories: Decentering the Object in Technoscience* (Durham, NC: Duke University Press, 2002a)

—— 'On Hidden Heterogeneities: Complexity, Formalism and Aircraft Design', in J. Law, and A. Mol, eds, *Complexities: Social Studies of Knowledge Practices* (Durham, NC: Duke University Press, 2002b), pp. 116–141

—— 'On the Subject of the Object: Narrative, Technology, and Interpellation', *Configurations*, 8 (2000), 1–29

—— *Organizing Modernity* (Oxford, UK and Cambridge, MA: Blackwell, 1994)

Lieberman, P., 'Imagination: Looking in the Right Place (and in the Right Way)', in J. Phillips, and J. Morley, eds, *Imagination and its Pathologies* (Cambridge, MA, and London: MIT Press, 2003), pp. 21–36

Mackenzie, C., and N. Stoljar, eds, *Relational Autonomy: Feminist Perspectives on Autonomy, Agency, and the Social Self* (Oxford and New York: Oxford University Press, 2000)

Macknight, V., 'Ideal Knowing: Logics of Knowledge in Primary School Curriculum', *British Journal of Sociology of Education*, 32.5 (2011a), 717–728

—— 'What is Relational Abstracting? The Case at Victorian Primary Schools', *Science as Culture*, 20.4 (2011b), 455–470

—— 'So, You Want to Feel at Home? Domesticating Australia in 1950s Primary Education', *Journal of Australian Studies*, 34.1 (2010), 49–61

—— 'For King, For Country: Changing "Good" Behaviour in Victoria, 1930s and 1950s', *Australian Journal of Politics & History*, 54.1 (2008), 55–68

—— 'Civics Education and Epistemology at Victorian Primary Schools, 1930s and 1950s', *History of Education Review*, 36.2 (2007), 46–60

Marres, N., 'Issues Spark a Public into Being: A Key but Often Forgotten Point of the Lippmann-Dewey Debate', in B. Latour, and P. Weibel, eds, *Making Things Public* (Cambridge MA: MIT Press, 2005), pp. 208–217

Maton, K., 'Languages of Legitimation: The Structuring Significance for Intellectual Fields of Strategic Knowledge Claims', *British Journal of Sociology of Education*, 21.2 (2000), 147–167

McGinn, C., *Mindsight: Image, Dream, Meaning* (Cambridge, MA and London: Harvard University Press, 2004)

McMillan, M., *Education Through the Imagination* (Bristol: Thoemmes Press, 1995)

Merleau-Ponty, M., *Maurice Merleau-Ponty: Basic Writings*, T. Baldwin, ed. (London and New York: Routledge, 2004)

Mimica, J., *Intimations of Infinity: The Mythopoeia of the Iqwaye Counting and Number System* (Oxford, New York and Hamburg: Berg, 1988)

Mol, A., 'Mind your Plate! The Ontonorms of Dutch Dieting Advice', *Social Studies of Science*, 43.3 (2012), 379–396

—— *The Logic of Care: Health and the Problem of Patient Choice* (Abingdon, Oxon and New York: Routledge, 2008)

—— *The Body Multiple: Ontology in Medical Practice* (Durham, NC: Duke University Press, 2002)

—— 'Ontological Politics: A Word and Some Questions', in J. Law, and J. Hassard, eds, *Actor Network Theory and After* (Oxford and Malden, MA: Blackwell Publishing and the Sociological Review, 1999), pp. 74–89

Mol, A., and M. De Laet, 'The Zimbabwe Bush Pump: Mechanics of a Fluid Technology', *Social Studies of Science*, 30.2 (2000), 225–263

Mol, A., and J. Law, 'Embodied Action, Enacted Bodies: The Example of Hypoglycaemia', in R. Valérie Burri, and J. Dumit, eds, *Biomedicine as Culture: Instrumental Practices,*

*Technoscientific Knowledge, and New Modes of Life* (New York and London: Routledge, 2007), pp. 87–107

—— 'Regions, Networks and Fluids: Anaemia and Social Topology', *Social Studies of Science*, 24.4 (1994), 641–671

Moore, R., *Education and Society: Issues and Explanations in the Sociology of Education* (Cambridge and Malden, MA: Polity Press, 2004)

Moore, R., and J. Muller, 'The Discourse of "Voice" and the Problem of Knowledge and Identity in the Sociology of Education', *British Journal of Sociology of Education*, 20.2 (1999), 189–206

Moore, R., and M. Young, 'Knowledge and the Curriculum in the Sociology of Education: Towards a Reconceptualisation', *British Journal of Sociology of Education*, 22.4 (2001), 445–461

Piaget, J., *The Child's Conception of Number* (London: Routledge and Kegan Paul, 1952)

Pickering, A., 'New Ontologies', in A. Pickering, ed., *The Mangle in Practice: Science, Society, and Becoming* (Durham, NC, and London: Duke University Press: 2008), pp. 1–14

—— *The Mangle of Practice: Time, Agency, and Science* (Chicago: Chicago University Press, 1995)

—— 'The Mangle of Practice: Agency and Emergence in the Sociology of Science', *American Journal of Sociology*, 99.3 (1993), 559–589

—— 'From Science as Knowledge to Science as Practice', in A. Pickering, ed., *Science as Practice and Culture* (Chicago: University of Chicago Press, 1992), pp. 1–26

Pinch, T., 'Reservations about Reflexivity and New Literary Forms, or Why Let the Devil Have all the Good Times?', in S. Woolgar, ed., *Knowledge and Reflexivity: New Frontiers in the Sociology of Knowledge* (London: Sage, 1988), pp. 178–197

Pope, R., *Creativity: Theory, History, Practice* (London and New York: Routledge, 2005)

Rundell, J., 'Creativity and Judgement: Kant on Reason and Imagination', in J. Rundell, and G. Robinson, eds, *Rethinking Imagination: Culture and Creativity* (London and New York: Routledge, 1994), pp. 87–117

Sak, U., 'About Creativity, Giftedness, and Teaching the Creatively Gifted in the Classroom', *Roeper Review*, 26.4 (2004), 216–222

Sartre, J.-P., *Imagination: A Psychological Critique* (Ann Arbor: University of Michigan Press, 1962)

—— *The Psychology of Imagination* (Secaucus, NJ: Citadel Press, 1948)

Savage, M., 'Contemporary Sociology and the Challenge of Descriptive Assemblage', *European Journal of Social Theory*, 12.1 (2009), 155–174

Sawyer, R. K., 'Creative Teaching: Collaborative Discussion as Disciplined Improvisation', *Educational Researcher*, 33.2 (2004), 12–20

Schwartzman, H., *Transformations: The Anthropology of Children's Play* (New York and London: Plenum Press, 1978)

Singer, D., and J. Singer, *Imagination and Play in the Electronic Age* (Cambridge, MA and London: Harvard University Press, 2005)

Smith, B. H., *Scandalous Knowledge: Science, Truth, and the Human* (Durham, NC: Duke University Press, 2005)

Sørensen, E., *The Materiality of Learning: Technology and Knowledge in Educational Practice* (New York: Cambridge University Press, 2009)

Star, S. L., and J. Griesemer, 'Institutional Ecology, "Translations" and Boundary Objects: Amateurs and Professionals in Berkeley's Museum of Vertebrate Zoology, 1907–39', *Social Studies of Science*, 19.3 (1989), 387–420

Star, S. Leigh, 'Power, Technologies and the Phenomenology of Conventions: On Being Allergic to Onions', in J. Law, ed. *A Sociology of Monsters: Essays on Power, Technology and Domination* (London and New York: Routledge, 1991), pp. 26–56

—— 'Leaks of Experience: The Link between Science and Knowledge?', in J. Greeno, and S. Goldman, eds, *Thinking Practices in Mathematics and Science Learning* (Mahwah, NJ: Lawrence Erlbaum Associates, 1988), pp. 127–146

Stewart, S., *Nonsense: Aspects of Intertextuality in Folklore and Literature* (Baltimore and London: Johns Hopkins University Press, 1978)

Sternberg, R., 'Introduction', in J. Kaufman, and R. Sternberg, eds, *The International Handbook of Creativity* (Cambridge: Cambridge University Press, 2006), pp. 1–9

—— *Education as a Force for Social Change: Lectures*, R. Lathe, and N. Whittaker, eds, (Hudson, NY: Anthroposophic Press, 1997)

—— *Rudolf Steiner: An Autobiography*, P. M. Allen, ed. (Blauvelt, NY: Rudolf Steiner Publications, 1977)

Stockley, D., 'Empathetic Reconstruction in History and History Teaching', *History and Theory*, 22.4 (1983), 50–65

Strathern, M., *Partial Connections* (Lanham, MD: Rowman and Littlefield, 1991)

Suchman, L., *Plans and Situated Actions: The Problem of Human-Machine Communication* (Cambridge and New York: Cambridge University Press, 1987)

Sutton-Smith, B., *The Ambiguity of Play* (Cambridge, MA and London: Harvard University Press, 1997)

van Heur, B., L. Leydesdorff, and S. Wyatt, 'Turning to Ontology in STS? Turning to STS through "Ontology"', *Social Studies of Science*, 43.3 (2012), 341–362

Verene, D. P., *Vico's Science of Imagination* (Ithaca, NY, and London: Cornell University Press, 1981)

Verran, H., 'The Telling Challenge of Africa's Economies', *African Studies Review*, 50.2 (2007a), 163–83

—— 'Metaphysics and Learning', *Learning Inquiry*, 1 (2007b), 31–39

—— 'The Educational Value of Explicit Non-Coherence', in D. Kritt, and L. Winegar, eds, *Education and Technology: Critical Perspectives, Possible Futures* (Lanham, MD: Lexington Books, 2007c), pp. 101–124

—— 'A Story about Doing "The Dreaming"', *Postcolonial Studies*, 7.2 (2004), 149–164

—— 'A Postcolonial Moment in Science Studies: Alternative Firing Regimes of Environmental Scientists and Aboriginal Landowners', *Social Studies of Science*, 32, 5.6 (2002), 729–762

—— *Science and an African Logic* (Chicago and London: Chicago University Press, 2001)

—— 'Staying True to the Laughter in Nigerian Classrooms', *The Sociological Review*, 47 (1999), 136–155

Vico, G., *The First New Science*, L. Pompa, ed. (Cambridge: Cambridge University Press, 2002)

Vygotsky, L., 'Imagination and Creativity in Childhood', *Journal of Russian and East European Psychology*, 42 (2004), 7–97

Walkerdine, V., 'Reasoning in a Post-modern Age', in P. Ernst, ed., *Mathematics, Education and Philosophy: An International Perspective* (London and Washington, DC: The Falmer Press, 1994), pp. 61–75

—— *The Mastery of Reason: Cognitive Development and the Production of Rationality* (London and New York: Routledge, 1988)

Williams, R., 'The Tenses of Imagination', *Writing in Society* (London and New York: Verso, 1991)

Ward, T., M. Patterson, and C. Sifonis, 'The Role of Specificity and Abstraction in Creative Idea Generation', *Creativity Research Journal*, 16 (2004), 1–9

Warnock, M., *Imagination* (London: Faber and Faber, 1976)

White, A., *The Language of Imagination* (Oxford and New York: Blackwell, 1990)

Whitehead, A., *The Power of Two: Memoirs of a Rudolf Steiner Teacher* (Blackheath, NSW: Golden Beetle Books, 2004)

Wilson, C., *Rudolf Steiner: The Man and his Vision: An Introduction to the Life and Ideas of the Founder of Anthroposophy* (Northamptonshire: Aquarian Press, 1985)

Wineburg, S., *Historical Thinking and other Unnatural Acts: Charting the Future of Teaching the Past* (Philadelphia: Temple University Press, 2001)

Woolgar, S., and J. Lezaun, 'The Wrong Bin Bag: A Turn to Ontology in Science and Technology Studies?', *Social Studies of Science*, 43.3 (2012), 321–340

Woolgar, S., and M. Ashmore, 'The Next Step: An Introduction to the Reflexive Project', in S. Woolgar, ed., *Knowledge and Reflexivity: New Frontiers in the Sociology of Knowledge* (London: Sage, 1988), pp. 1–11

Woolley, J., 'Thinking about Fantasy: Are Children Fundamentally Different Thinkers and Believers from Adults?' *Child Development*, 68.6 (1997), 991–1011

Young, M., 'From Constructivism to Realism in the Sociology of the Curriculum', *Review of Research in Education*, 32.1 (2008), 1–28

# MATTERING PRESS TITLES

*On Curiosity*
*The Art of Market Seduction*

FRANCK COCHOY

*Practising Comparison*
*Logics, Relations, Collaborations*

EDITED BY
JOE DEVILLE, MICHAEL GUGGENHEIM AND ZUZANA HRDLIČKOVÁ

*Modes of Knowing*
*Resources from the Baroque*

EDITED BY
JOHN LAW AND EVELYN RUPPERT

*Imagining Classrooms*
*Stories of Children, Teaching, and Ethnography*

VICKI MACKNIGHT

www.ingramcontent.com/pod-product-compliance
Lightning Source LLC
Chambersburg PA
CBHW032351280326
41935CB00008B/526